IMAGES
of America

# WATAUGA COUNTY

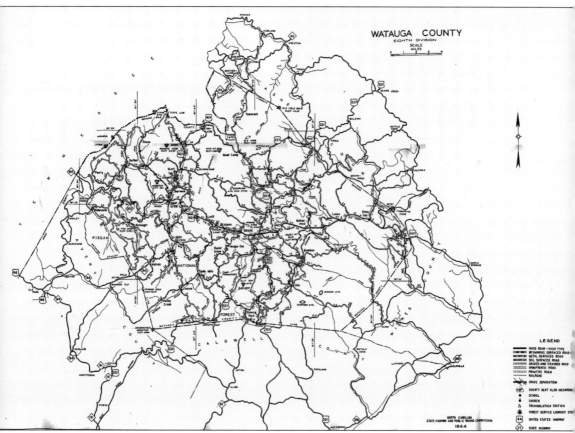

**MAP OF WATAUGA COUNTY, 1944.** This map was created by the North Carolina State Highway and Public Works Commission. Roads, railroads, schools, churches, and so on are visible in this image. (Courtesy of Marianna Eggers Isaacs.)

**ON THE COVER: ET&WNC.** Posing in front of an engine of the Eastern Tennessee and Western North Carolina Railroad (ET&WNC) and the depot building are, from left to right, Grover Miller (conductor), L. H. Herrell (baggage master), Sherman Pippin (engineer), a Mr. Perkins (who sold candy and gum on train), Earl Vest (fireman), W. R. Greene (city policeman), and Richard Johnson (depot agent). (Courtesy of Faye Greene.)

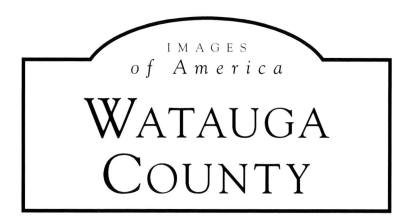

IMAGES
*of America*

# WATAUGA
# COUNTY

Donna Gayle Akers
and Brian Lambeth

ARCADIA
PUBLISHING

Published by Arcadia Publishing
Charleston, South Carolina

Printed in the United States of America

Library of Congress Catalog Card Number: 2008929805

For all general information contact Arcadia Publishing at:
Telephone 843-853-2070
Fax 843-853-0044
E-mail sales@arcadiapublishing.com
For customer service and orders:
Toll-Free 1-888-313-2665

Visit us on the Internet at www.arcadiapublishing.com

*From Donna: To all those who have
come before us who saved our history.*


*From Brian: To my mother; it is likely her fault
that I have such a fascination with history.*

# CONTENTS

# ACKNOWLEDGMENTS

It is fortunate that the large developments in Watauga County happened when photography was available. In this book, you will find never-before-published, as well as some previously published, photographs of places and people that add to the corpus of Watauga County's history. Watauga County, as evidenced by these photographs and images, is rich in history and uniqueness. It is the hope of the authors that you create a little of your own history in the county; the beauty of the county cannot responsibly be placed into print—it must be seen.

This book would not have been possible without the contributions of the following people and organizations: Faye Green, J. P. Greene, Historic Boone, the Valle Crucis Conference Center, Mariànna Eggers Isaacs, Byron and Sharon Tolbert, Richard Trexler, Nannie Greene, Ned Trivette, Warren Greene, Jason Reagan, the *Watauga Democrat*, Jane Penley, Robert and Virginia Mann of the Todd General Store, Ted Mast, Stacy Eggers Jr., Margaret Eggers, Glenda Baird Vance, Sarah Lynn Blair Spencer, Becca Eggers-Gryder, Wayne Sumner, the Watauga County Public Library, and the photographers and record keepers of the past whose works were left unreferenced due to limited documentation. Thanks goes out to all of you.

# INTRODUCTION

"We saw hundreds of mountain peaks all around us, presenting a spectacle like ocean waves in a storm," is how the area that later became Watauga County was described by Bishop August Gottlieb Spangenberg, leader of the first group of explorers to the region in 1752. The mountains here are some of the oldest in the world. Natural processes over time have created a smooth, flowing, and somewhat accessible topography.

The area that is now Watauga County was long ago the domain of the Cherokee tribe. Their abundant remains of pottery, stone tools, and arrowheads are evidence of their existence. None of the first explorers in the mid-1700s encountered Native Americans. It remains a mystery as to why the Cherokee tribe abandoned the area so long ago.

Daniel Boone made regular trips to the area beginning sometime before 1761. He trail blazed through the area by means of an old buffalo trail that is now called the Daniel Boone Trail. The first settlers to the county were composed of the same groups that settled the foothills to the east: English, German, and Scotch-Irish pioneers. Evidence suggests that the first permanent settlements were in the Valle Crucis area beginning around 1780. Many of the first settlers were veterans of the American Revolutionary War, which by this time, had come to an end. The first federal census in 1790 describes an increasing population.

Jordan Councill Jr. operated a store in what is now the town of Boone that attracted other businesses around it. It quickly became a hub of commerce. Around 1823, a U.S. Post Office, commonly called "Councill's Store," was established in that same area. The popularity and size of Councill's Store eventually caused Boone to be named the county seat. On January 27, 1849, Watauga County was created by the General Assembly of North Carolina by mostly appropriating land from Ashe, Caldwell, Wilkes, and Yancey Counties. The first courthouse was constructed in 1850 on land donated by Jordan Councill Jr. The county's population in 1850 was 3,348. Ten years later, the population would be 4,957, an increase of about 50 percent.

When the American Civil War began, the majority of citizens were loyal to the South, and the county provided about 1,000 soldiers to the Confederacy. As the war progressed, more and more swayed to side with the Union, and the county furnished about 100 soldiers to the Union Army.

Following the Civil War, the county's one major issue was transportation. The county belonged to an area known as "the Lost Provinces." Transportation to the area from other parts of North Carolina was almost impossible. It was said that the only way to get to Watauga County was to be born there. Features of this isolated economy included subsistence farming and underfunded public schools because there was little tax revenues. Citizens pushed for a railroad as early as 1852. Finally, in 1917, the Eastern Tennessee and Western North Carolina Railroad (ET&WNC) made its way through the county. Toll and state funded roads sprang up around the county. The isolation of this "Lost Province" was finally broken. The flood of 1940 washed away most of the railroad tracks, but by this time, hard-surfaced roads were so prevalent that the need for a railroad was eliminated.

Along these conduits came students, commerce, and tourists. Appalachian State University, once a school for training teachers, saw increasing enrollment as the need for teachers across the state increased. Private academies such as the Valle Crucis Mission School, Cove Creek Academy, and New River Academy flourished. Commercial farming boomed in the 1920s and is mostly attributable to the new roads. Chief crops included corn, wheat, rye, oats, hay, potatoes, tobacco, and cabbage. As Bishop Spangenberg first noted, the natural beauty of the county is undeniable. The county rapidly became a tourism destination based on this beauty alone. The final chapter of this book displays many of the different activities available to visitors.

# *One*

# LANDSCAPES

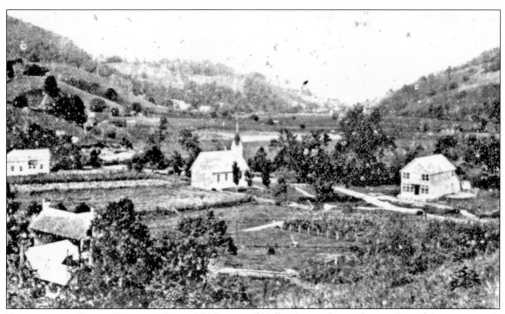

DOWNTOWN VALLE CRUCIS. This c. 1900 view of Valle Crucis shows the vitality of this crossroads town. A bank is shown on the left of the photograph along Highway 194, and the Methodist church is standing in the center and is still there today. The large building on the right of the photograph is the Farthing store, which is now the Mast Store Annex. The Mast Store, which is also a post office, is not visible but is located across Broadstone Road from the church. (Courtesy of Valle Crucis Conference Center.)

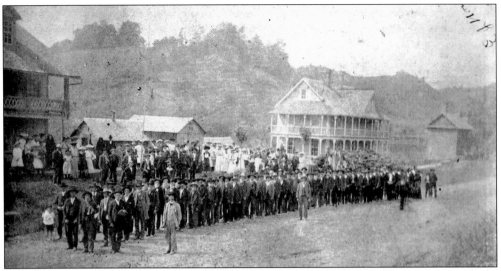

**E. J. NORRIS.** Norris is pictured in this *c.* 1906 photograph of downtown Boone. This view looks west down what is now King Street. The building at the far right is the Watauga Democrat office. Next to it on the right is the W. L. Bryan residence. The building on the far left is the Blair Hotel. Note that the streets are not hard surfaced, and no power lines exist. The photographer was standing in front of the J. D. Councill house, where the Boone Post Office stands today. (Courtesy of Faye Greene.)

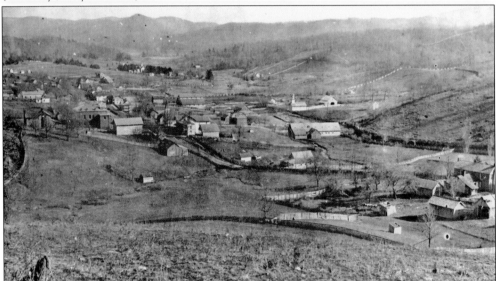

**BOONE DOWNTOWN, 1903.** The town of Boone is depicted here in mid-winter, and the lower and upper slopes of the mountains seem to have been logged and converted for farmland. Fences outline the property lines of farms and neighbors. The old Watauga County courthouse is shown in the center left of the photograph, while across the street is the Methodist church. The two-story brick house with smoke rising from the chimney (on the lower right of the photograph) was owned by Judge L. L. Greene. His wealth is evident by the numerous outbuildings and several horses. The Coffee barn is the linear, white, frame building in the middle right of the photograph. The white frame church with the steeple on today's Rivers Street is the Boone Baptist Church, which was built in 1873. (Courtesy of Historic Boone.)

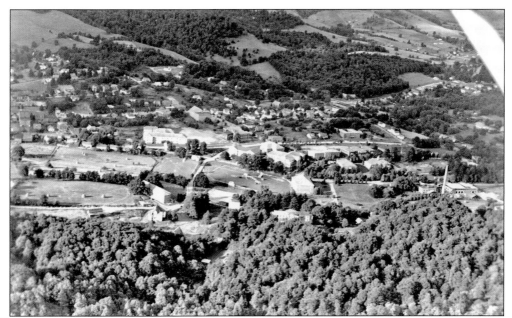

**A.S.T.C. AERIAL.** Something interesting is happening on the Appalachian State Teachers College football field (middle center) of this 1949 photograph. *Echoes of the Blue Ridge*, the predecessor of *Horn in the West*, was staged on the football field around this time. Today's I. G. Greer Hall (middle right, above the steam plant) has not yet been constructed, but the ground has been broken. (Courtesy of Brian Lambeth.)

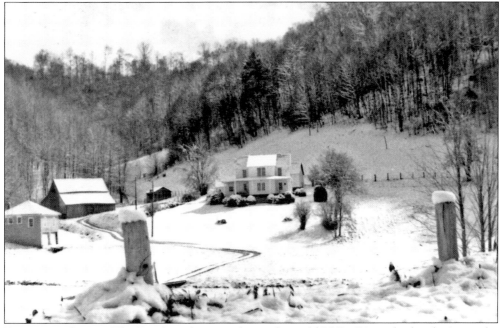

**BINGHAM HOUSE.** The Bingham house is located on old U.S. 421 in the lovely Amantha community. Once a bustling community with a gristmill, descendents of the Binghams still live in the house and farm the land. Today Amantha is a peaceful residential community. (Courtesy of Marianna Eggers Isaacs.)

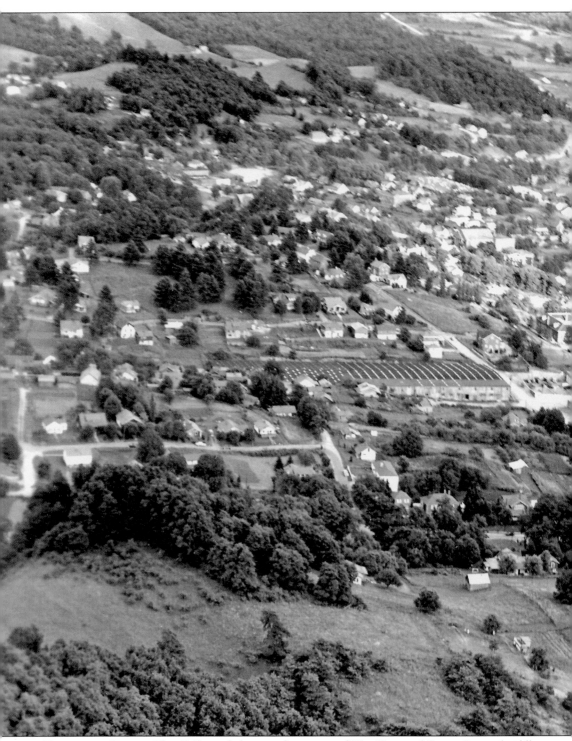

**DOWNTOWN BOONE.** This 1949 aerial photograph is a view of West King and Queen Streets (middle center) in downtown Boone, the Appalachian State Teachers College (top center), and Blowing Rock Road (very top center). Buildings of interest include the Watauga County courthouse (bottom right),

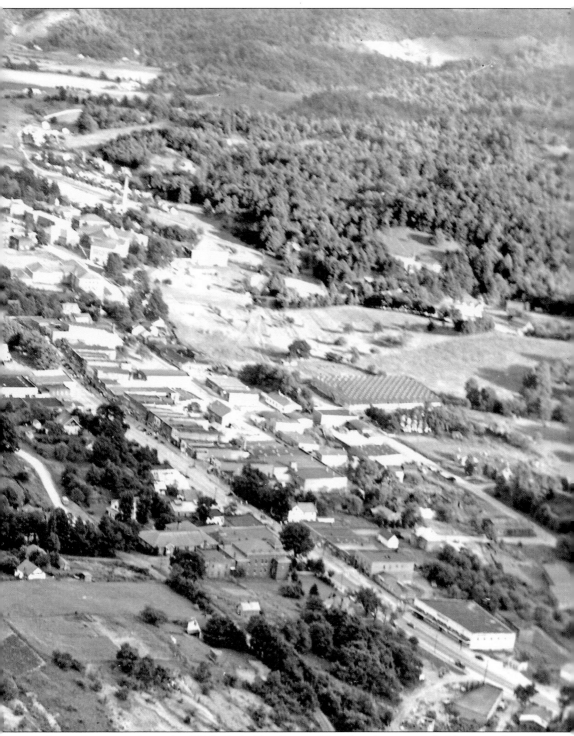

a large tobacco warehouse (middle left), the First Baptist Church without a steeple (above warehouse along King Street), and the adjacent Methodist church. (Courtesy of Brian Lambeth.)

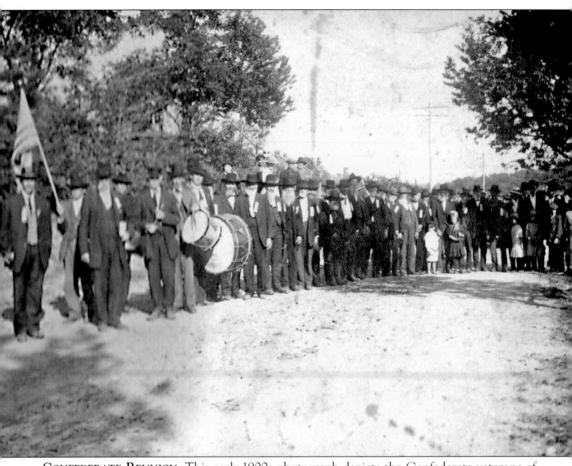

**CONFEDERATE REUNION.** This early-1900s photograph depicts the Confederate veterans of Watauga County. Almost 1,000 men from Watauga County fought for the Confederates, while only 100 men joined the Union troops. Elijah Norris is present in the photograph. (Courtesy Faye Greene.)

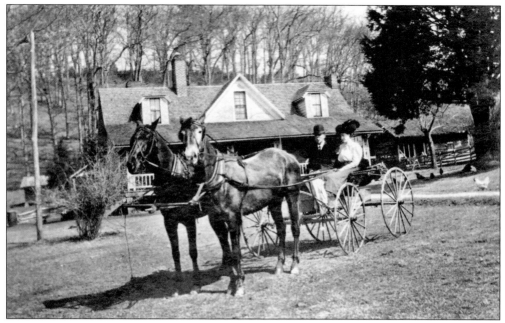

**HENRY BLAIR FARM.** Julius Rousseau Blair and his wife, Anne Gordon Shearer, are riding in a carriage around 1915. The Blair House, built in 1844 by Henry Blair, is visible in the background. The house once sat upon 365 acres, along with orchards, livestock, and grain fields. The house, several outbuildings, and yielding farmland remain in use today. The estate is actively being preserved by descendants of Henry Blair. (Courtesy of Historic Boone and Byron and Sharon Tolbert.)

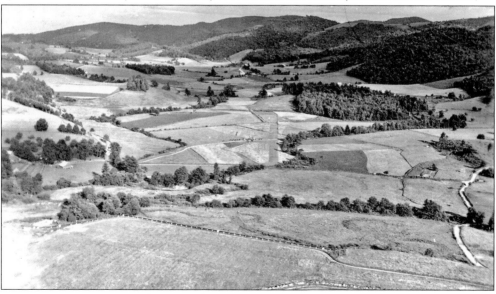

**BAMBOO AREA, 1949.** Lovely hay fields and cattle pastures are located just to the east of Boone in the Bamboo area. This setting is what the Blair House (pictured above) would have been seated upon. The production of hay at this time surpassed that of any other single crop. Dairy farming was on the rise in 1949. Five dairies were operating in the county in 1940, and, in 1949, one hundred dairies were in operation, and many more were under construction. (Courtesy of Brian Lambeth.)

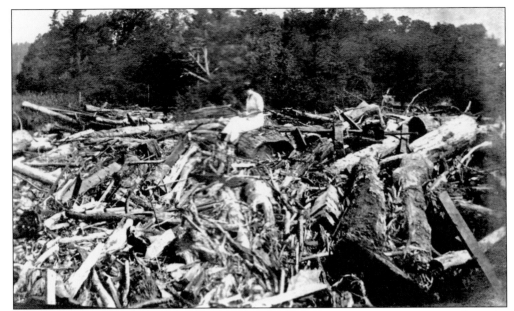

**FLOOD DEBRIS.** The third hurricane of the 1940 season, a category-one storm, brought about the August 13, 1940, flood to Watauga and adjoining counties. Sixteen people within the county perished as a result of the flood. Florence Blair Ballew is shown seated on top of an enormous pile of debris near Boone that includes whole trees and lumber from houses. (Courtesy of Byron and Sharon Tolbert.)

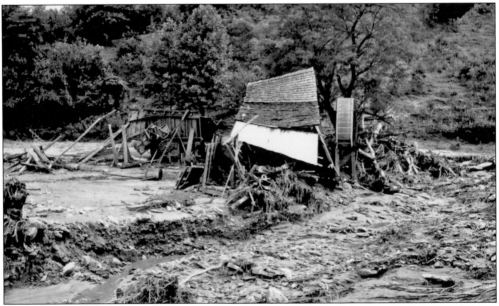

**FLOOD-DAMAGED MILL.** Water-driven mills, by nature, can only operate near courses of water. Lawrence Greene operated this small creek-driven mill near Deep Gap, North Carolina. The house and mill were once adjacent. Greene was in the house at the time and witnessed the entire mill separating from the house and moving downstream. The heavy rains had caused the ground to become so saturated that the soil moved like a liquid and caused the stable portions to tremble. (Courtesy of Richard Trexler.)

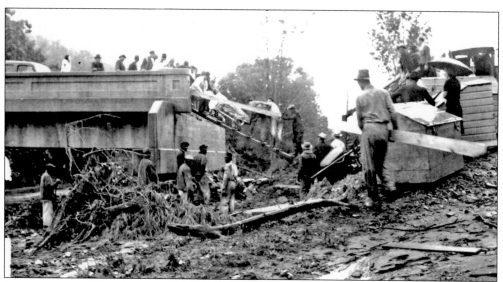

**FLOOD RESCUE.** This photograph, taken following the flood, might have been at the household of Andrew Greene. Four people in the household died, and three survived. Ivery C. Greene's book, *A Disastrous Flood*, mentions two trips to Watauga Hospital for the survivors. B. L. Greene was one of the survivors not hurt. The book reads, "[Eliza Greene] was changed by the flood, being so badly bruised about the face that [Ernest Greene] did not recognize her. He carried her the home where she was treated with kind solicitude by everyone in the family and made ready to be taken to Watauga Hospital." In another passage, the book reveals a second rescue that reads, "The next morning [Hooper Greene] was taken to the Watauga Hospital in Boone, where he underwent treatment for three days."(Courtesy of Richard Trexler.)

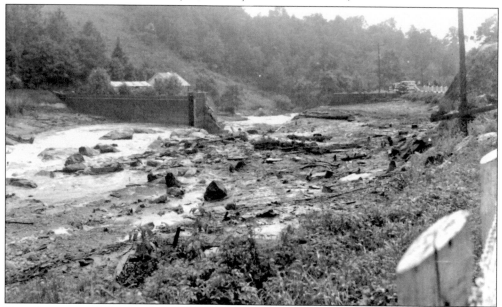

**DAM REMNANTS.** The flood devastated all four Shulls Mill dams along the Watauga River. The dams provided electricity to more than 1,000 households and housed the largest power station in the county at the time. Remnants of one of the dams are visible today from Shulls Mill Turnpike Road. (Courtesy of Richard Trexler.)

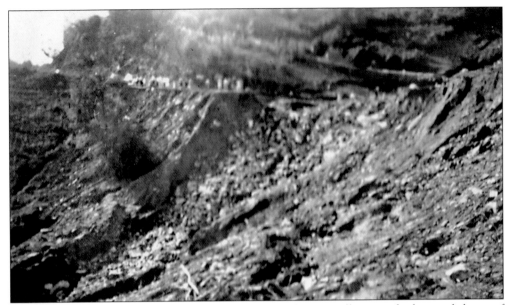

**ERASED LANDSCAPE.** Roads were usually built along the naturally created edges and slopes of the mountains. The deep-rooted trees that once preserved the slope were no more. After raining nonstop for more than a week, the ground in the area was completely saturated. Without the binding power of vegetation, the potent mixture of water and gravity caused roads to be erased from the edges of slopes. (Courtesy of Richard Trexler.)

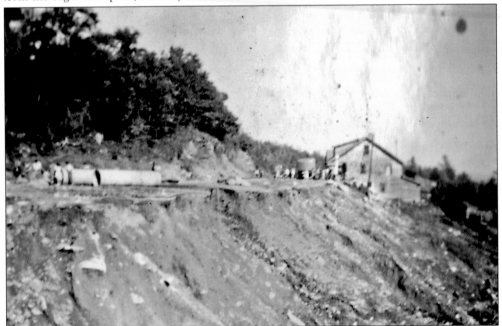

**RECONSTRUCTION.** A still fresh-looking landslide has been graded along the top edge so that a road can be rebuilt. Concrete drainage pipes to divert a stream under the roadway are visible on the left. The dark area along the side of the slope indicates water flow. The photograph dates to just after the flood since no vegetation exists in the slope area and the leaves have not fallen. (Courtesy of Richard Trexler.)

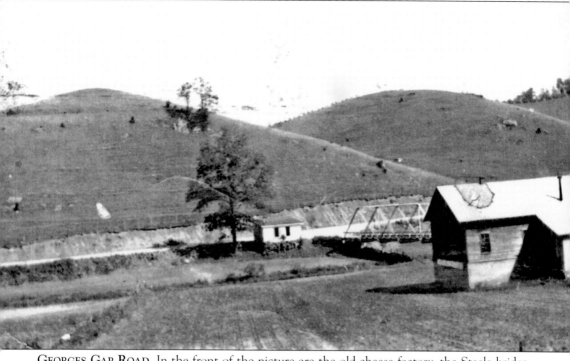

**GEORGES GAP ROAD.** In the front of the picture are the old cheese factory, the Steele bridge, and Sugar Grove Post Office. Barely visible is the Walnut Grove School on top of the hill in the middle of the photograph. (Courtesy of Nannie Greene.)

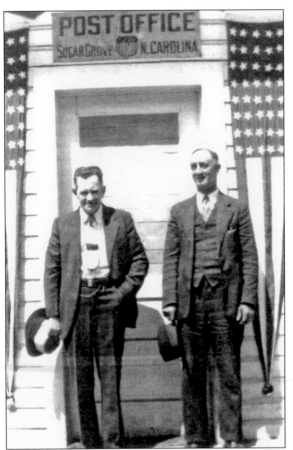

**SUGAR GROVE POST OFFICE.**
Vardry Mast (left) and route carrier
Bill Banner are pictured in front
of the Sugar Grove Post Office.
Banner delivered mail on horseback
but later used an automobile.
(Courtesy Nannie Greene.)

**SUGAR GROVE SCENE, 1933.**
The Clyde and Jennie Mast house
(below), built 1929–1930, is shown
in the front of the photograph, and
the Moose Club's Snow Lodge is in
the background. The large white
house belonged to John Bingham.
(Courtesy of Nannie Greene.)

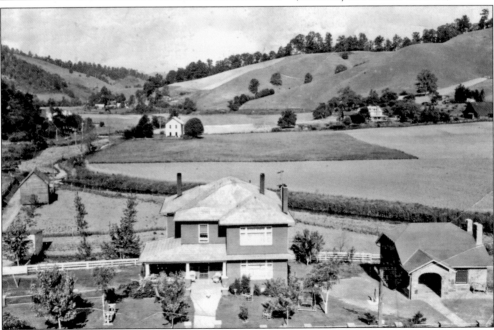

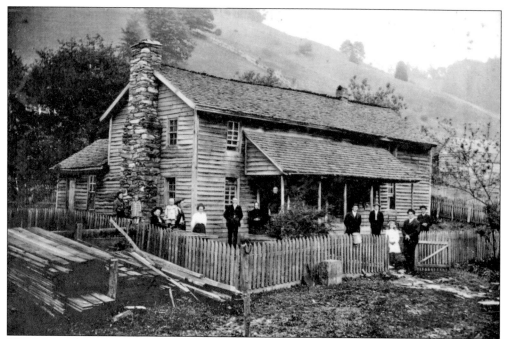

**MOUNTAIN FRAME CONSTRUCTION.** Stone chimneys, wooden shingles, and clapboards defined the typical mountain home at the beginning of the 20th century. All components of the house were produced by sawmills in the area. Lumber was an abundant and cheap resource. This house is unidentified and dates to around 1910. (Courtesy of Historic Boone.)

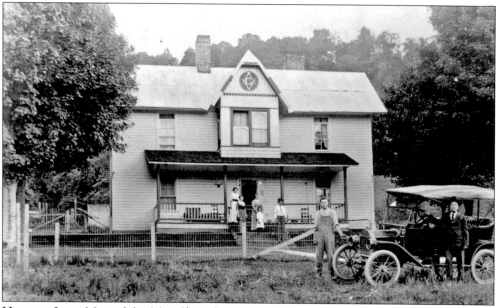

**HOME OF JOHN MAST.** John Mast (far right, next to car) is photographed in 1915 with his newly acquired 1914 Ford. Farmhand Clyde Corum is standing to the left of car. On the steps, from left to right, are Nettie Greer (boarding with John and Nan Cleo Mast, wife of Clarence J. Mast), unidentified, Nan Mast, Nora Mast (the youngest child of Pete Mast), and Clarence J. Mast (the oldest child of Pete Mast). A Masonic symbol is featured on the home's dormer. (Courtesy of Historic Boone.)

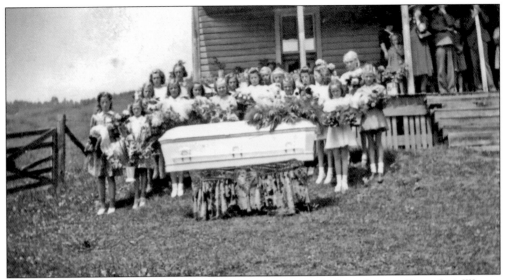

**FUNERAL.** Pictured here is a child's funeral, a sad but common sight from the past. Young Lois Warren was a student at Bethel Elementary School who died of leukemia, and her school class gathered to mourn her passing. (Courtesy of Ned Trivette.)

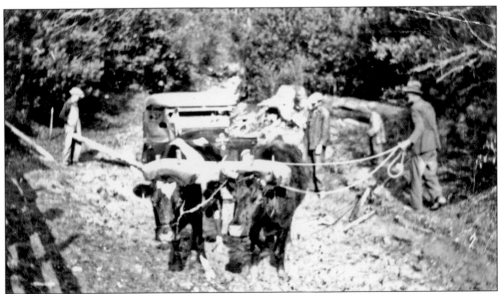

**EARLY OXEN TOW.** The back of the photograph reads, "A car stuck in the mud—red clay—at Deep Gap N.C. 1929 in April. A Tarheel hauling tan bark nearby went to his rescue with the Oxen, I was on a log train, had engineer stop and let me make this picture, The yoke of steers walked right off with the car." No train ran through Deep Gap; the location of this photograph is likely in Todd or west of Boone. (Courtesy of Brian Lambeth.)

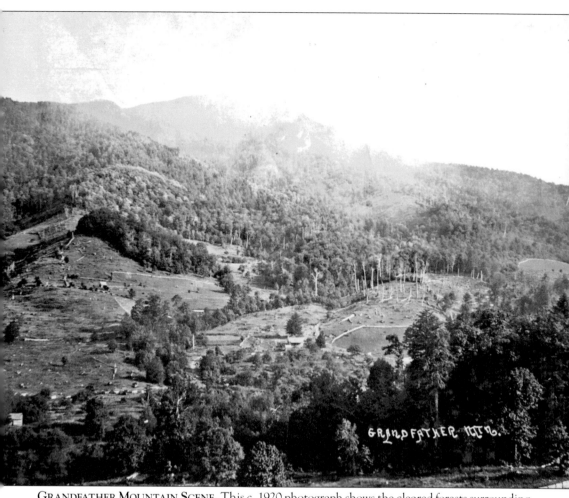

**GRANDFATHER MOUNTAIN SCENE.** This *c.* 1920 photograph shows the cleared forests surrounding Grandfather Mountain. By this time, the ET&WNC chugged to the northwest of Grandfather Mountain. Lumbering operations were in full swing all along the tracks that headed to Tennessee. Most old-growth forests were cleared. (Courtesy Historic Boone.)

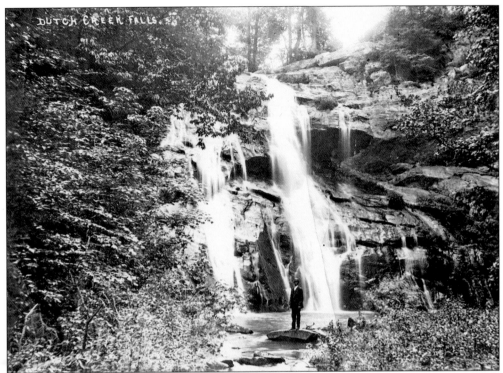

**DUTCH CREEK FALLS.** *Watauga* is said to be a Native American word for "beautiful water." This 1920s photograph of the "beautiful water" of Dutch Creek is located in Valle Crucis. Waterfalls are prevalent in the area. A similar waterfall can be viewed today near the Valle Crucis Conference Center. (Courtesy of Historic Boone.)

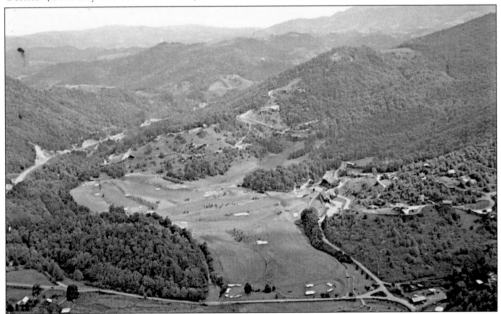

**HOUND EARS CLUB.** This early view of the Hound Ears Club shows the distinctive shape of the two mountains and some of the houses. (Courtesy of Richard Trexler.)

# *Two*

# AGRICULTURE

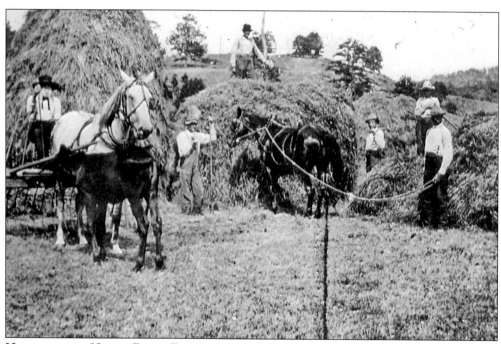

**HAYSTACKS AT HENRY BLAIR FARM, C. 1910.** Before gathering hay, the tall grasses were cut with a scythe at maturity and allowed to dry in the fields. It was then raked into narrow rows, called windrows, using a horse-drawn hay rake. Hay is photographed here in the final process, where it is being gathered and stacked. Stacks were built in such a way that they would shed water to prevent mold and rot. The man (far left) sitting on the hay rake is George Henry Blair (1847–1916). He was the youngest son of Henry Blair, the builder of the Blair House, and the second owner of the farm. George's son, Henry Neal Blair, is standing on the hay in the center of the photograph and was the father of the photographer, Palmer Blair. (Courtesy of Historic Boone and Byron and Sharon Tolbert.)

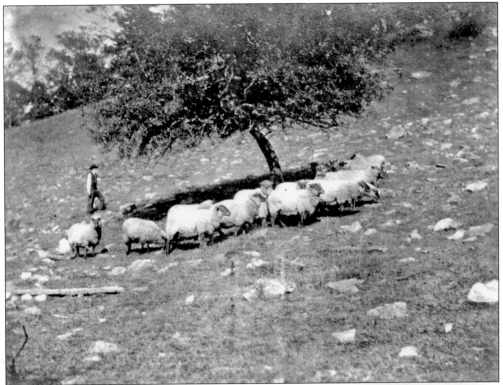

**SHEEP.** Suffolk sheep, raised primarily for meat, appear here in a field on the Blair Farm around 1910. The sheep industry in the county peaked in the 1950s then declined as the demand for wool and mutton decreased. George Henry Blair is shown leading the flock around a fruit tree. (Courtesy of Byron and Sharon Tolbert.)

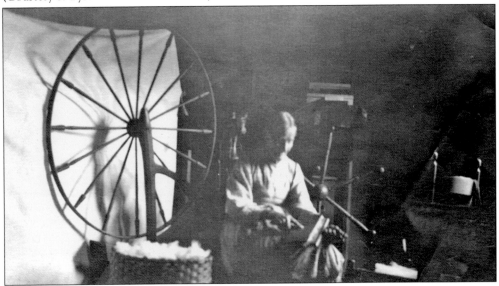

**CARDING WOOL.** Susan Farthing (1833–1922) is shown carding wool for spinning in the Dudley Farthing house on Beaverdam in this c. 1900 photograph. The Dudley Farthing farm was largely self-sufficient by design. (Photograph by James C. Shell, courtesy of J. P. Greene.)

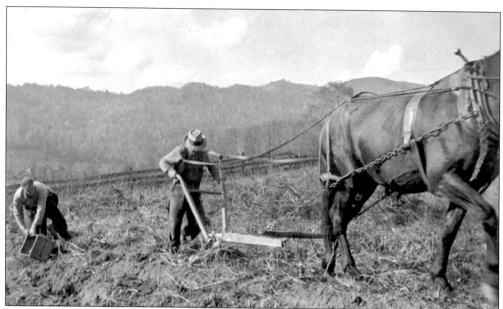

PLOWING BY HORSE. A draft horse is pulling a plow pushed by an employee of the Valle Crucis School. The school grounds provided much of the food for the students. (Courtesy Valle Crucis Conference Center.)

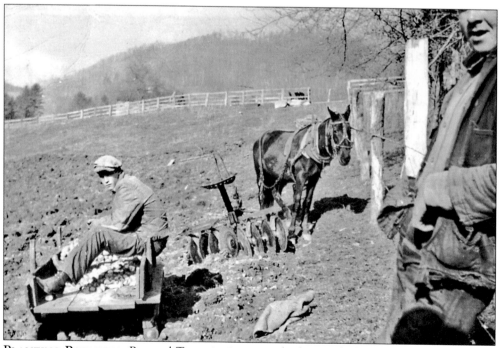

PLANTING POTATOES. Bernard Tester is sitting in the box with the potatoes ready to plant while Raymond Hollar is resting against the fence at the Valle Crucis School. Potatoes were a mainstay of the residents' diet and were commonly cultivated on area farms. (Courtesy of Valle Crucis Conference Center.)

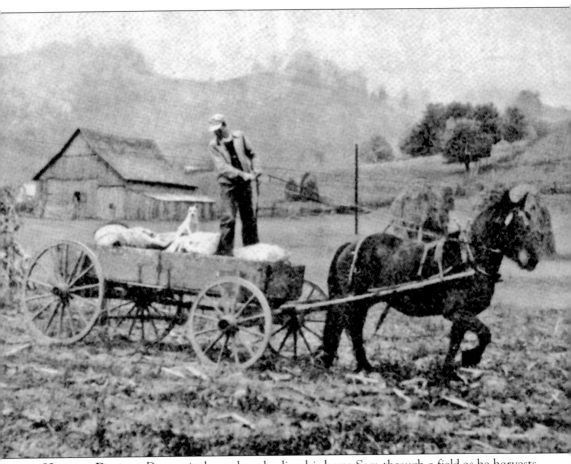

**HOWARD DANCEY.** Dancey is shown here leading his horse Sam through a field as he harvests corn from the W. R. Billings farm in Vilas. He was born on September 18, 1918, in the Silverstone community of Watauga County. He was a farmer and carpenter, and was enlisted by the U.S. Army during World War II. Later Dancey ran Dancey's Shoe Store adjacent to the Flowers Photo Shop on King Street. He purchased it in 1970 with his wife, Ivalee. This 1940s photograph of Howard Dancey was used on the cover of the October 1960 issue of *Adult Teacher*, a Southern Baptist Sunday school education booklet. (Courtesy of Historic Boone.)

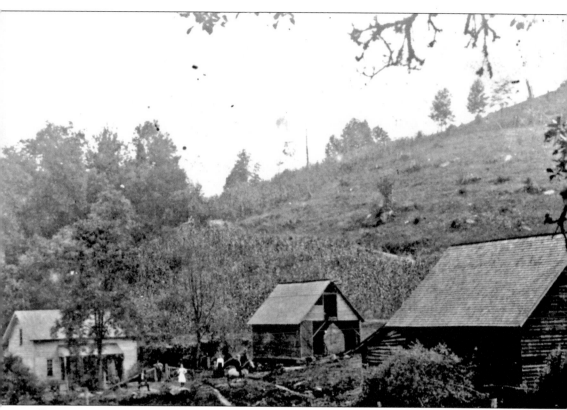

**HAGAMAN FARM.** Representative of a typical Appalachian farmstead is the Dan Hagaman farm, which was located on Zion Hill. From the left to right are Ed Hagaman, unidentified, Susie Hagaman, Mary Harmon Farthing Hagaman, and Hardy Hagaman (sitting on the horse). The frame farmhouse is on the left, the corncrib is in the middle, and the large barn is on the right in the photograph. (Courtesy of Ned Trivette.)

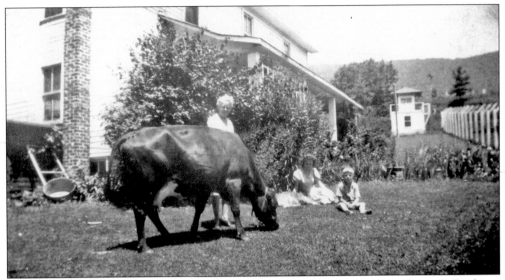

**FARTHING FAMILY, C. 1943.** Maude Lee Farthing, wife of superintendent Carter J. Farthing, is pictured with daughter Dorothy Farthing Greene and grandson Hal Buckner Farthing Jr. on the grounds of the prison camp on Hodges Gap Road about 1943. This area is now home to the Watauga County Law Enforcement Center. The materials from the demolished superintendent's house were recycled into the chapel building. (Courtesy of J. P. Greene.)

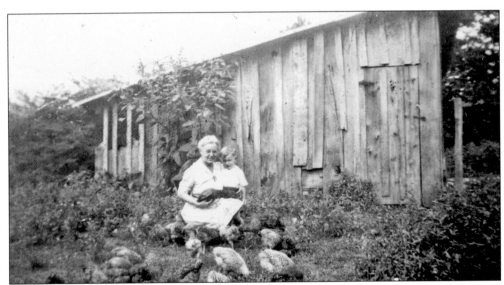

**FARTHING FARM.** Maude Lee Farthing (1894–1983) is shown with her youngest son, Harrison Winfield Farthing (1934–?) at the chicken house on the Farthing farm in Bethel about 1938. Although a symbol of the past today, every farm kept its own chicken house for eggs and poultry. (Courtesy of J. P. Greene.)

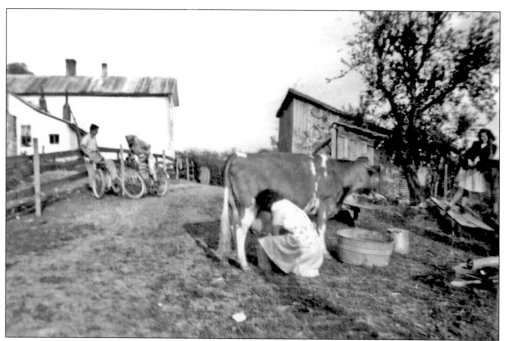

**MILKING.** Celia Ward is milking a cow at the Greene family home and farm on Peoria Road. Ned Trivette (far left) and Grayson Ward are standing with bikes along the fence. Mary Trivette is standing on the far right in the photograph. (Courtesy Ned Trivette.)

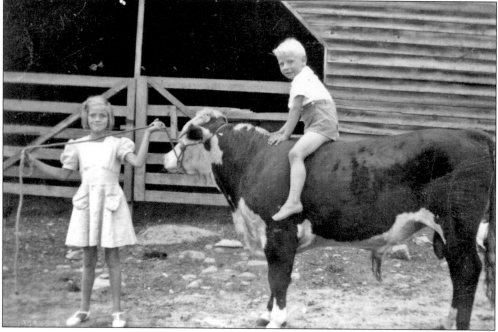

**NORRIS'S PRIZE BULL.** Robbie Lynn Norris and brother Dudley Norris are posed proudly with their prize bull in this c. 1945 photograph. Beef cattle production increased in the 1940s as farming techniques improved the production of hay and the quality of the bloodlines. Several meatpacking companies were located around Boone. (Courtesy of J. P. Greene.)

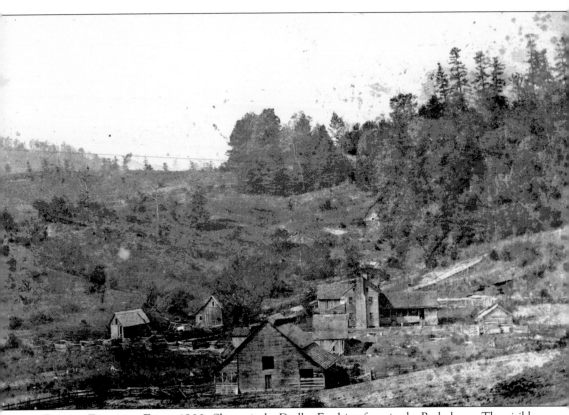

**DUDLEY FARTHING FARM, 1900.** Shown is the Dudley Farthing farm in the Bethel area. The visible buildings, listed from left to right, are the stable, servant's house, barn (which is still standing), chicken house, wood shed, main house, and smokehouse. Dudley Farthing (1804–1895) was an original settler and was the first judge of the Court of Pleas and Quarter Sessions in Watauga County. At the time this photograph was taken, the farm was owned by his unmarried daughter Susan (1833–1922) and was operated by his grandson Dudley Farthing Greene (1879–1957). The site is on John Shell Road, located about one-fourth of a mile north of Bethel Road. (Courtesy of J. P. Greene.)

# *Three*

# CHURCHES AND SCHOOLS

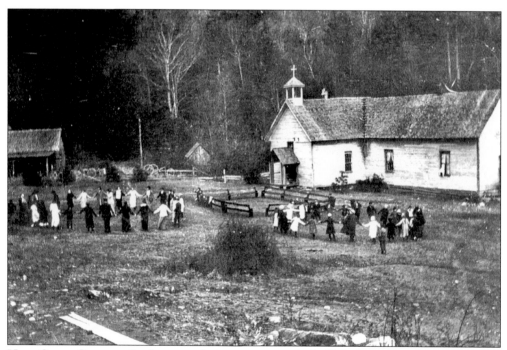

HOLY CROSS CHURCH. Students are playing games outside the Holy Cross Church on the grounds of the Valle Crucis School in the early 1900s. A section of the church remains and is used as a meeting space near the apple barn. The early presence of the church in this small Valle Crucis community brought benefits such as schools, education, jobs, religious services, and assistance to the residents. (Courtesy of Valle Crucis Conference Center.)

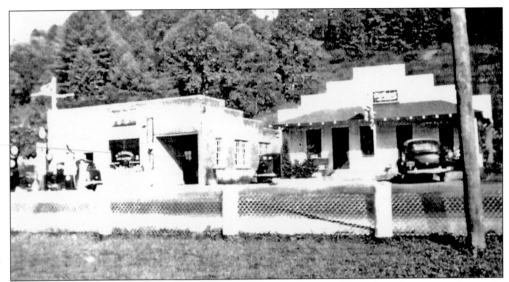

**COVE CREEK BAPTIST CHURCH.** The Cove Creek Baptist Church is shown in this early photograph. Used by the community from 1881 to 1923, the church was also used periodically by the Walnut Grove School and Cove Creek Academy. It was replaced by a new brick church. (Courtesy of Nannie Greene.)

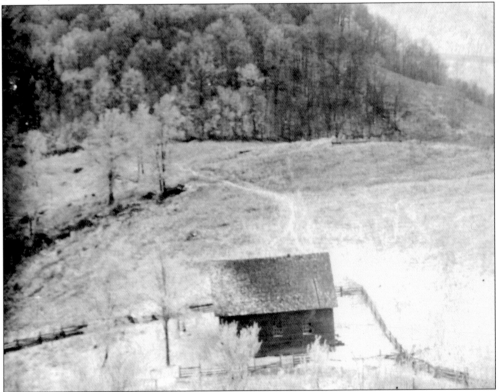

**ZION HILL CHURCH.** Originally known as the "Windie Gap Church," this was the earliest Zion Hill Church. This small frame building was later replaced with a new brick church that is still standing on U.S. 321. (Courtesy of Ned Trivette.)

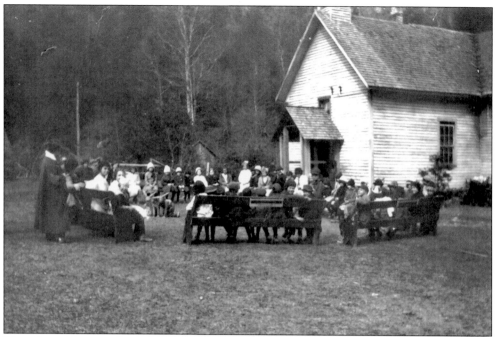

HOLY CROSS CHURCH. Students at the Valle Crucis day and boarding school are seated on pews listening to a minister at the Holy Cross Church. (Courtesy of Valle Crucis Conference Center.)

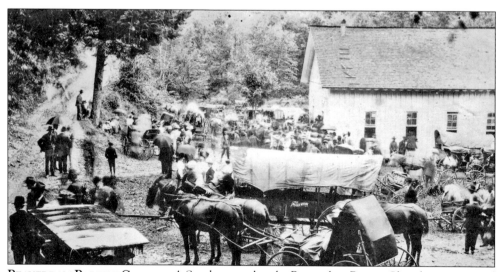

BEAVERDAM BAPTIST CHURCH. A Sunday crowd at the Beaverdam Baptist Church was captured in this *c.* 1905 photograph by James C. Shell. Note the Nissen Wagon emblem on the wagon in the center. The Nissen Wagon Works was based in Winston-Salem, North Carolina, and provided many of these once ubiquitous conveyances to the area. (Courtesy of J. P. Greene.)

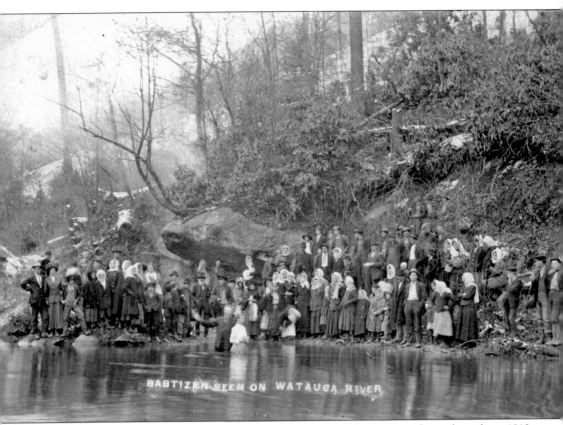

BABTIZEN SEEN ON WATAUGA RIVER

**BAPTISM.** In hypothermia-inducing conditions, a wintertime baptism is taking place about 1910 in the Watauga River. Modern weather statistics reveal that the average temperature of the Watauga River in January is 34 degrees Fahrenheit. According to the *Didache*, or *Teaching of the Twelve Apostles*, a book written in about 100 A.D. that details the administration of a baptism, the event is to take place in "living" water (i.e. running water) at its natural temperature. Partial immersion or submersion was the dominant mode of baptism in the early church. The preference for baptisms in rivers can be attributed to the baptism of Jesus in the River Jordan. (Courtesy of J. P. Greene.)

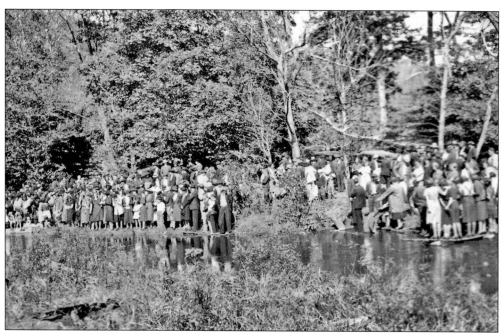

**HOWARD'S CREEK BAPTIST CHURCH.**
Located on Howard's Creek, baptisms were conducted in the waters as shown in this early-1900s photograph (above). The church was constituted in 1882 and soon joined the Three Forks Baptist Association in 1883. The first church building was constructed soon afterwards, and Sunday school first began here in 1884 with 60 pupils. (Courtesy Warren Greene.)

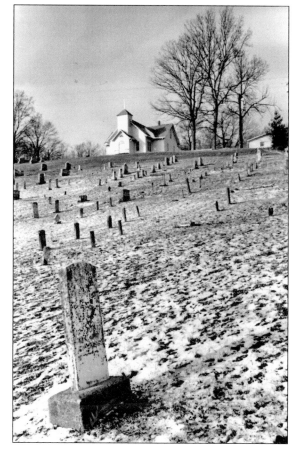

**MEAT CAMP BAPTIST CHURCH.** The Baptist Church was first established in Meat Camp, North Carolina, in 1851. The church immediately joined the Three Forks Baptist Association. This particular wood-framed church was constructed in the 1920s and is still in use today. Brick was used in the construction of most of the new churches by the 1940s. (Courtesy of *Watauga Democrat* and Historic Boone.)

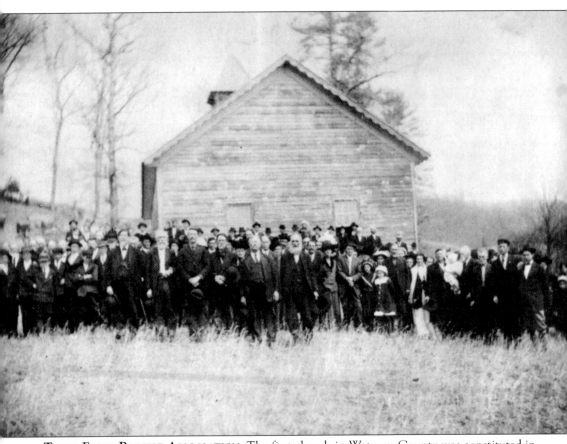

**THREE FORKS BAPTIST ASSOCIATION.** The first church in Watauga County was constituted in 1790 and was named the Three Forks Baptist Church. The log church was built on the bank of the New River. Cove Creek Baptist was the second church in the county when it was constructed in 1799. These two churches formed the basis of the association in 1840. In 1851, the Bethel Baptist Church was added, followed by Beaverdam's Baptist in 1874. In "The Winning of the West" by Theodore Roosevelt, the following quote is made about churches in Watauga County around 1894: "the preachers and congregations, alike, went armed, the latter leaning their rifles in their pews or near their seats, while the pastor let his stand beside the pulpit." Pictured here is a meeting of the association held at the Bethel Baptist Church around 1900. (Courtesy of *Watauga Democrat*.)

**TIMBERED RIDGE CHURCH.** The original Timbered Ridge Church was built in 1906 on Peoria Road and is still standing today. The congregation is shown leaving Sunday service in this 1940s photograph. (Courtesy of Ned Trivette.)

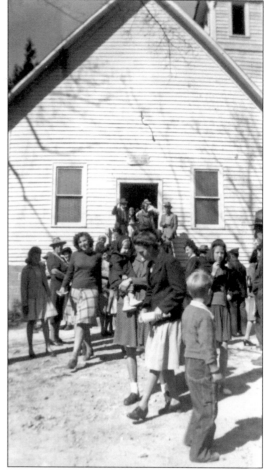

**CHESTNUT GROVE SCHOOL.** This one-room school (below) was located in the Chestnut Grove area but is no longer standing. The only identified students in this photograph are, from left to right, the following: (first row) Beatrice Jones, Ola Greene, and Laura Foster; (second row, beginning third from left) Beonie Hodges, James Forester, and Dave Lewis; (third row) Ike Lewis, Bonard Greene, and sixth from the left is Lester Jones. (Courtesy of Warren Greene.)

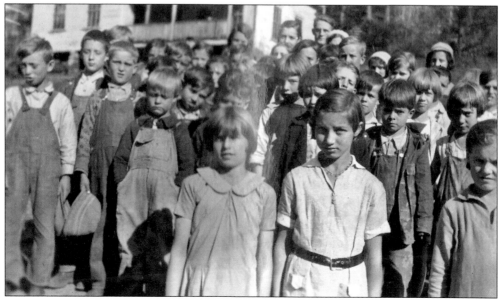

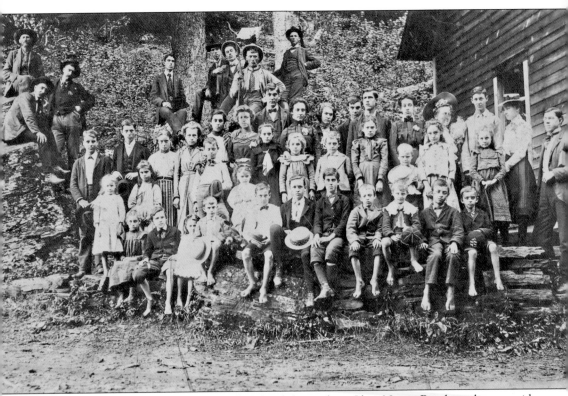

**SANDS SCHOOL.** The one-room Sands School, located on Clint Norris Road on the west side of N.C. Highway 194 is shown here in about 1900. Students in the photograph include (in no particular order) Elijah Norris, Bill Norris, Newton Barnes, Coy Miller, Jack Norris, John Hodges, Conley Brown, Ona Trivette, Gurney Norris, Mollie Norris, Maggie Norris, Bill Hayes, Addie Norris Ragan, Paul William, Lettie Hayes, Minnie William, Bessie Barnes, Ben Greene, Rubin Miller, Lillie Williams, Blanch Williams, Thomas Hayes, Emma Story, Bob Wall, and Thomas Roscoe Brown. (Courtesy of Faye Greene.)

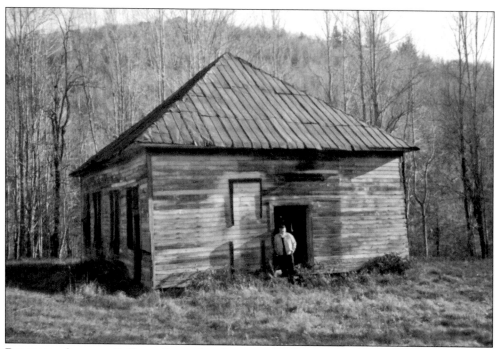

**ROMINGER SCHOOL.** Still standing today, the one-room Rominger School served many pupils in the area. Susie Hagaman Trivette was a teacher there. (Courtesy of Ned Trivette.)

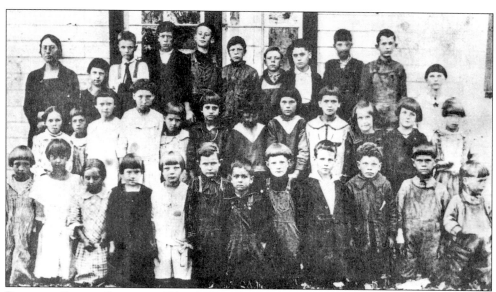

**ROMINGER SCHOOL STUDENTS.** Taken by W. R. Trivett, this c. 1922 photograph shows a serious group of students at the Rominger School. Many of the children bear evidence of the "bowl cut," when a bowl was placed over their heads and used to cut the hair straight. (Courtesy of Ned Trivette.)

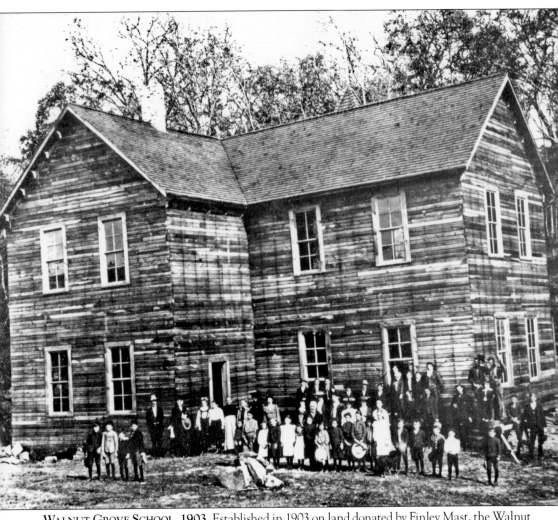

**WALNUT GROVE SCHOOL, 1903.** Established in 1903 on land donated by Finley Mast, the Walnut Grove School was located on Old Meeting House Hill. The school was built by subscriptions from local families. This two-story frame school served many Cove Creek students for years until it was consolidated with Cove Creek Academy and the Phillips School to form the Cove Creek Elementary School. John H. Bingham is the teacher on the left of the photograph. The sessions at these rural schools often followed the planting and harvesting seasons, and the school years were not always nine months long. (Courtesy of Nannie Greene.)

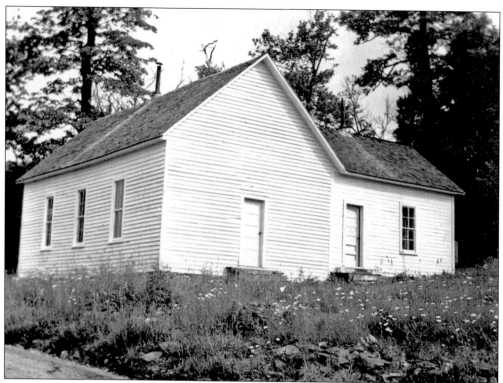

**RICH MOUNTAIN SCHOOL.** First opened in 1890, this one-room schoolhouse was in use until it was consolidated into Green Valley in 1950. Students in approximately the first through seventh grades were taught here. (Courtesy of Jane Penley.)

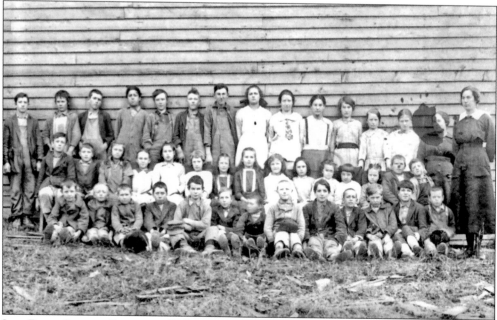

**IVEY RIDGE SCHOOL STUDENTS.** W. R. Trivett took this school photograph of students at Ivey Ridge, a one-room school. The school was located on Rush Branch Road. (Courtesy of Ned Trivette.)

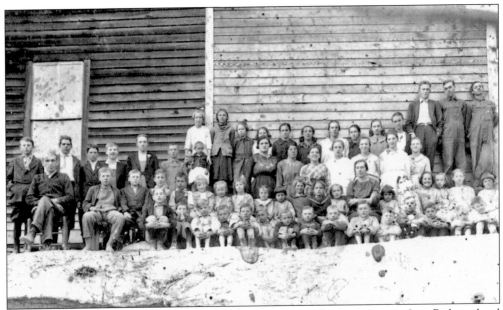

IVEY RIDGE SCHOOL STUDENTS. These students pose outside the one-room Ivey Ridge school building. Roby Vines is the teacher sitting on the left, and Susie Hagaman, the other teacher, is sitting in the second row. (Courtesy Ned Trivette.)

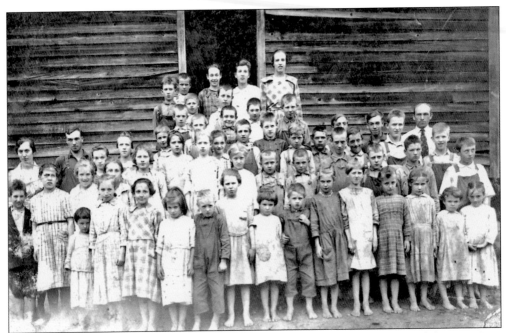

IVEY RIDGE SCHOOL STUDENTS. These young students are standing in front of the one-room Ivey Ridge school building, which was located on Rush Branch Road. Susie Hagaman (teacher) is standing on the left, and Roby Vines (teacher) is standing on the right of the photograph. (Courtesy Ned Trivette.)

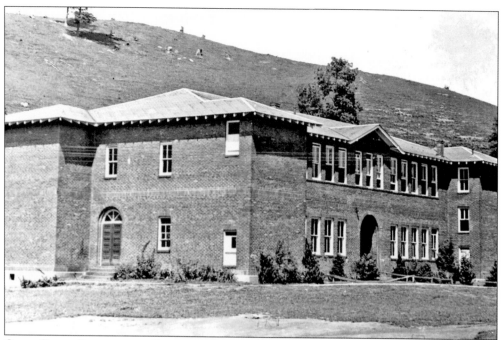

COVE CREEK ELEMENTARY SCHOOL. This school was built in 1922 and served all grades with Glenn Greer as the principal. Cove Creek combined the pupils of Cove Creek Academy, Walnut Grove Institute, and the Phillips School. Replaced by a stone building, the brick buildings were later demolished. (Courtesy Nannie Greene.)

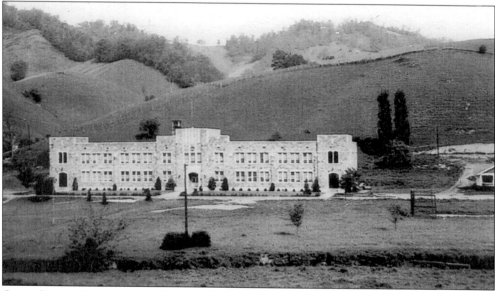

COVE CREEK HIGH SCHOOL. Built in 1941 as a Works Progress Administration project, Cove Creek High School remained the local high school until it was consolidated in 1965. Shop space, the gymnasium, and the auditorium were provided by the old school building located adjacent to the new school. Robert Shipley and the school's agricultural department operated a cannery, which provided affordable, safe canning for local farmers. Today the Western Watauga Community Center occupies the building. (Courtesy Nannie Greene.)

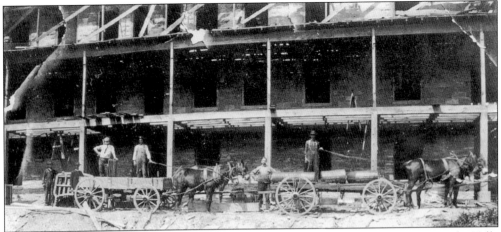

**ACHMUTY HALL CONSTRUCTION.** Achmuty Hall, now the Inn, is being built *c.* 1908 at the Valle Crucis Conference Center. Horses and mules pull wagons loaded with construction materials to build this spacious, lovely building. The building serves as the inn for the conference center. (Courtesy of Valle Crucis Conference Center.)

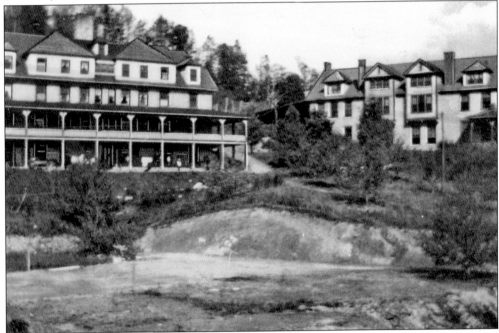

**ACHMUTY HALL AND ANNEX.** Achmuty Hall is shown on the left, and the Annex is on the right in this *c.* 1910 photograph of the Valle Crucis Conference Center. In 1842, Bishop Levi Ives began an Episcopal church ministry in Valle Crucis. In 1903, the Episcopal church bought part of Bishop Ive's property and developed the school into a flourishing institution. Improvements included apple orchards, a dairy, a sawmill, a wagon factory, and a hydroelectric power plant, as well as new, larger buildings. In 1936, the school became a girls' boarding high school but still accepted community girls. Due to shortages during the war, in 1943, the school was closed and was only used for a summer training program for seminary students and a summer inn. In the 1960s, the property and many of the original buildings became the Episcopal Church Conference Center. (Courtesy Valle Crucis Conference Center.)

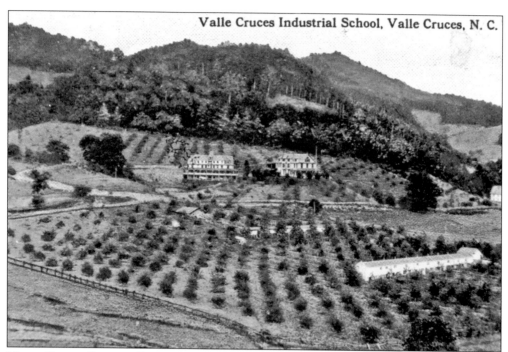

**VALLE CRUCIS SCHOOL CAMPUS.** Apple orchards run across the fields in front and behind the Achmuty Hall and the annex. The long building in the foreground is a chicken barn. (Courtesy of Valle Crucis Conference Center.)

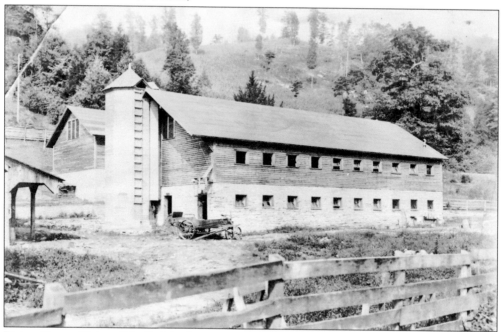

**DAIRY BARN.** This well-built dairy barn served its purpose at the Valle Crucis School. With its sturdy construction and stone foundation, it was built in 1911 to last for many years. A small apple storage barn is behind the barn. Today it is known as the "Apple Barn," and it serves as a community gathering place. (Courtesy of Valle Crucis Conference Center.)

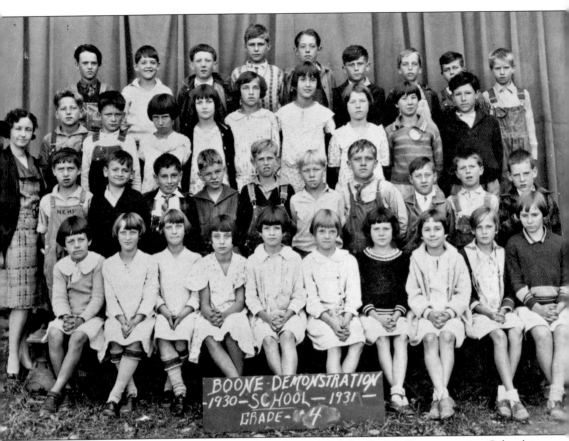

**BOONE DEMONSTRATION SCHOOL.** The fourth grade of the Boone Demonstration School is pictured in 1930–1931. From left to right are (first row) Geneva Greer, Bessie Gragg, Jessie Gragg, Carsia Mae White, Elouise Wilson, Elizabeth South, Ruth Issacs, Dell Bush, Mary Margaret Idol, and Margaret Hollar; (second row) J. D. Cook, Jack Williams, Junior Greene, Fred Wyte, Tom Wright, Boyd Norris, Truett Greer, Buck Vandyke, James Norris, and Jack Triplett; (third row) Hunter Storie, Glenn Teams, Jenna Lee Bingham, Ruby Wellborn, Edna Ragan, Virginia Hayes, Louise Setzer, Mary Snow Brown, and Otto Watson; (fourth row) Jack Miller, James Greer, Arlow Watson, J. W. Beach, Arthur Tripplett, Leige Hollar, Maston Norris, Brian Shull, and Warren Greene. The teacher is a Miss Flemming from Ashe County. (Courtesy of Warren Greene.)

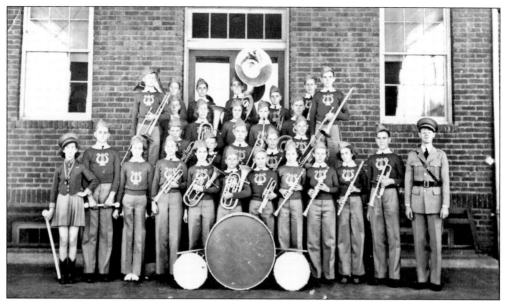

**BOONE HIGH SCHOOL BAND.** The school band is photographed here in late 1938. The drum major, complete with whistle and large baton, is on the far left. Palmer Blair is immediately to the right of the drum major. Gordan Nash, also a professor at Appalachian State at the time, is on the far right. (Courtesy of Historic Boone.)

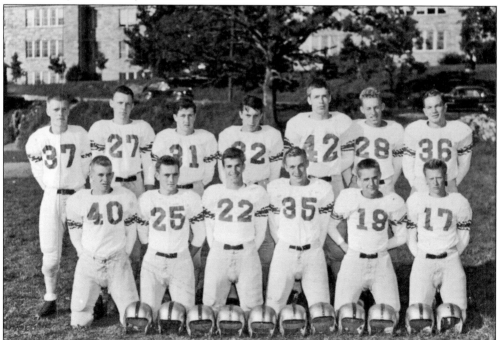

**A.H.S. BLUE DEVILS, 1953.** The 1953 Appalachian High School football team is shown here. Pictured from left to right are (first row) Donald Lyons, Armfield Coffey, Charles Taylor, Harbin Moretz, Jim Brown, and John Norris; (second row) Kermit Ashley, Bill Talbert, Charles Winkler, Bill Jones, "Little" Guy Hunt, Jimmy Idol, and Bobby Ray. Appalachian High School is visible in the background. (Photograph by *Watauga Democrat*, courtesy of Historic Boone.)

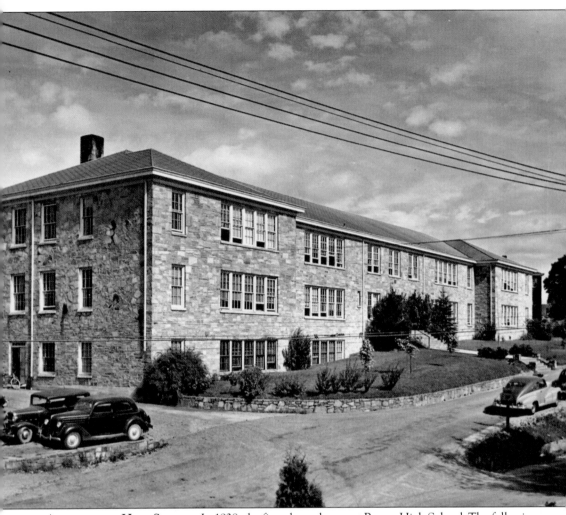

**Appalachian High School.** In 1938, the first classes began at Boone High School. The following year it would be renamed to Appalachian High School. The school was located on the campus of Appalachian State Teachers College and served as a training school for student teachers. In 1939, the high school had an enrollment of approximately 340 students. Features of the building included a lunchroom, a large auditorium, a gymnasium, a reading room, and a library with more than 2,000 books. The school was under the supervision of the director of teaching training, who was then Chapell Wilson. High school classes here ended in 1965 when the five area high schools were consolidated into one. The building itself is still in use today by Appalachian State University as Chapell Wilson Hall. (Courtesy of Historic Boone.)

# *Four*

# BUSINESS AND INDUSTRY

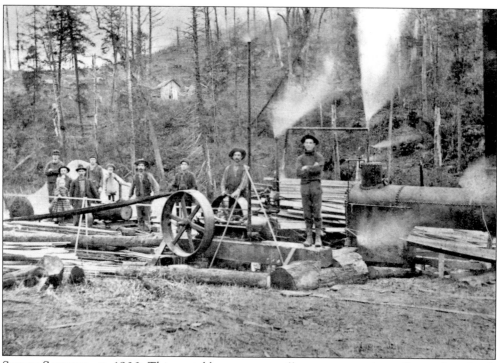

**STEAM SAWMILL, C. 1900.** This portable steam sawmill was set up on lower Beaverdam Creek in what is now the Bethel community. The mill's owner, Wiseman Cable (standing at the flywheel) was a well-known logger and sawmiller in the area well into the 1920s. Appearing in the photograph are James C. Shell, (1864–1937) photographer, standing between his two children Crathie (1895–197?) and James E. Shell (1897–196?); and Dudley F. Greene (1879–1957), later a prominent farmer, standing by the boiler. Some of the others may be Wiseman Cable's sons, who were in business with him. At the time of the photograph, hundreds of these small mills were active in Western North Carolina, producing railroad ties and fine hardwoods for furniture and millwork. Lumber was hauled by wagon to railheads in Lenoir and Neva, Tennessee. Shortly after this photograph was taken, Dudley Greene spent two years in the Tacoma, Washington, area working in logging and sawmilling before returning to marry in 1905 and to raise his family. Johnny Greene (1915–1992) and his brother Edgar (1912–1990) told of making the two-day trip by themselves from Beaverdam to Neva over Baker's Gap with a wagonload of lumber many times in the 1920s. (Courtesy of J. P. Greene.)

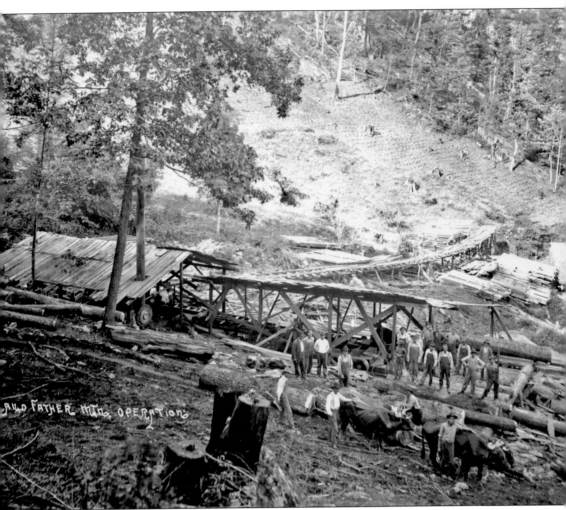

**GRANDFATHER MOUNTAIN SAWMILL.** It can be said that the first major industry in Watauga County was the lumber business. The only sawmills that existed in the county before railroads were introduced were used to provide lumber for construction locally. Three sawmills operated near Boone around 1850 for this purpose. When railroads were constructed through the county during World War I, financial success came to those who could produce and trade lumber. This c. 1920 photograph shows a steam-powered sawmill operation. Tree trunks were loaded (bottom right) by a small railcar system into the sawmill (left). Rough-sawn boards were then sent down the steep ramp and then stacked at the base of the mountain. Note the child laborer, oxen pulling logs by chain, and the railcar transporting sawn lumber away from the premises. (Courtesy of Historic Boone.)

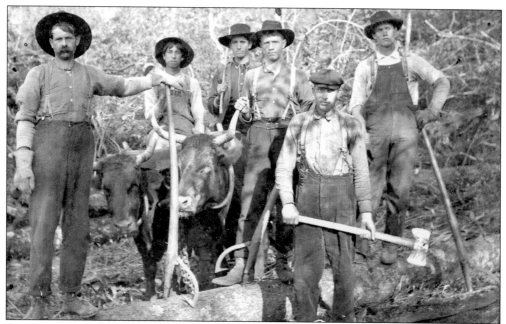

LUMBERING. These men were cutting trees and rolling them down the mountain. W. R. "Roby" Greene is the man standing with an ax in his hand. Two oxen were used to pull the logs down. (Courtesy of Faye Greene.)

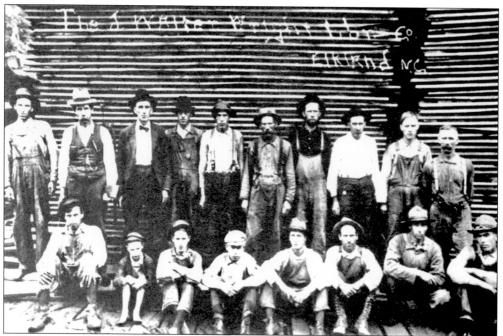

FREIGHT LUMBER. Workers of the J. Walter Wright Lumber Company, a company based in Spruce Pine, are pictured in front of rough-sawn lumber bound for Virginia in this c. 1915 photograph. The Virginia Creeper Railroad ran from Abingdon, Virginia, to Elkland, North Carolina (now Todd, North Carolina), transporting primarily lumber to Virginia. A few workers in the first row appear to be children. (Courtesy of Todd General Store.)

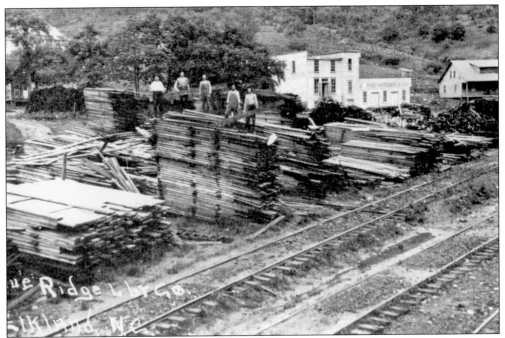

**VIRGINIA CREEPER TRACKS.** Elkland, now Todd, was the terminus of the Virginia Creeper Railroad in 1915. As a result, a once-small community expanded to a bustling town that catered to passengers, railway workers, and lumber dealers. The Todd Mercantile Company, the brighter building at the top right, was built in 1910 in anticipation of the business that the railroad would bring. (Courtesy of Todd General Store.)

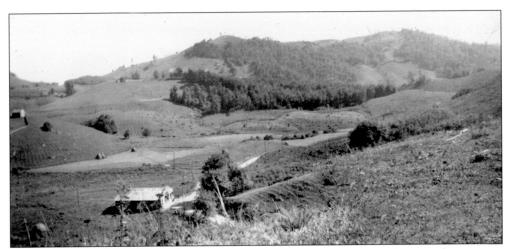

**CLYDE PERRY STORE.** This 1942 photograph shows the Clyde Perry Store and surrounding scenery in Bethel. Dyer Knob is visible on the right side. The knob is a prominent peak in Bethel and nearby Sugar Grove with an elevation of 3,420 feet. Note the haystacks in the fields. (Photograph by Johnny P. Greene Sr., courtesy of J. P. Greene.)

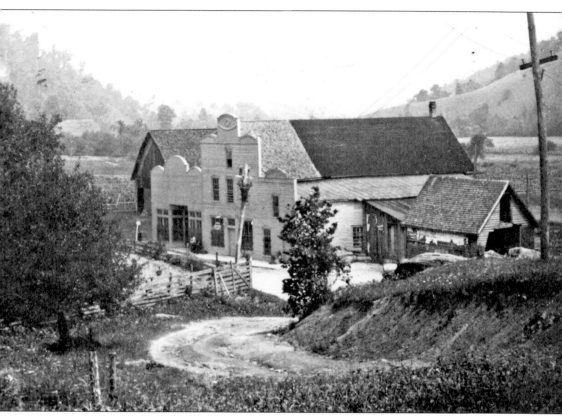

**MAST GENERAL STORE, VALLE CRUCIS.** Henry Taylor built this general store in 1882 amidst the growing community of Valle Crucis. It was not until 1897, when employee William Wellington Mast took part ownership of the store, that the name became the "Taylor and Mast General Store." In 1913, W. W. Mast purchased Taylor's share in the business, and the name of the store changed to what it is today. Three generations of Masts would own and operate the store, until 1973, when it was sold away from the family. The store later changed hands for a final time in 1980 to John and Faye Cooper. The store carried a wide assortment of items for its customers. One of the advertisements read, "Goods for the living; Coffins and caskets for the dead." (Courtesy of Richard Trexler.)

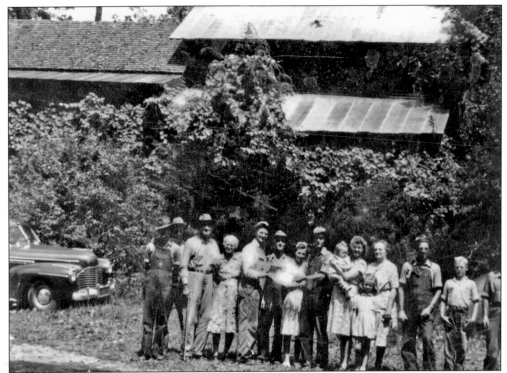

**MAST AND HORTON FAMILY.** This 1930s photograph was taken at the Cove Creek School area off Vanderpool. From left to right are two unidentified, Watt Henson (a farmer), wife Maggie Henson, Don Horton (the first veterinarian in Watauga County), Don Henson, Edith Henson, Jack Henson, four unidentified, Robert Mast, Bobby Mast, and unidentified. (Courtesy of Ted Mast.)

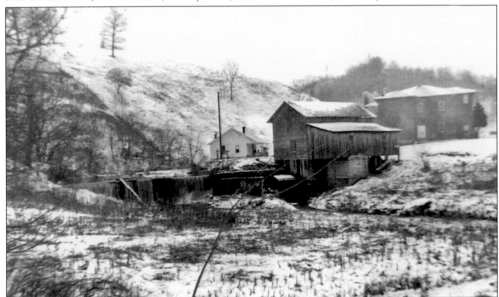

**GRISTMILL, 1940S.** This gristmill at Cove Creek was owned by Dan Stokes, and Hensel Stokes was the miller. He lived in the adjacent white house. The old Cove Creek Elementary School is shown in the background. (Courtesy of Nannie Greene.)

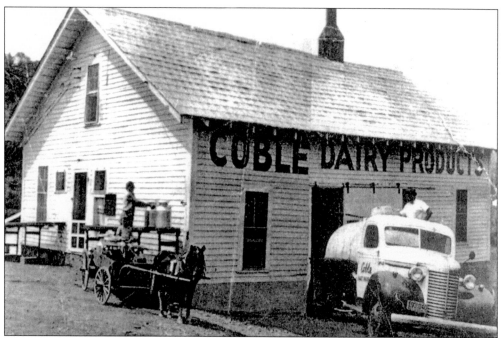

**COBLE DAIRY.** The Coble Dairy in Sugar Grove replaced the cheese factory and gave local farmers a market for their milk. Bill Stokes delivered this neighbor's milk to the dairy with the help of five-year-old David Campbell. (Courtesy Nannie Greene.)

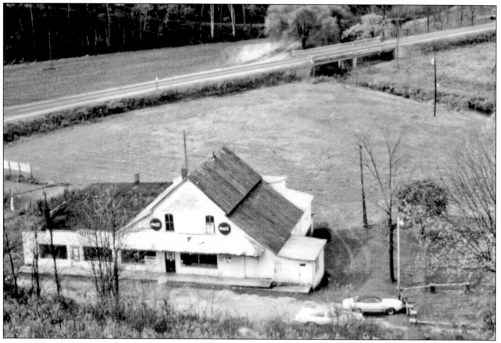

**A.C. MAST STORE, 1983.** Today, as in the past, the frame-store building looks much the same. Once stores such as this were located at most crossroads. It is now used as a residence. (Courtesy of Nannie Greene.)

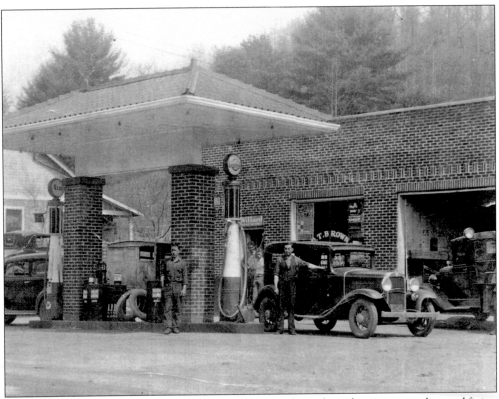

**DEWITT BROWN'S GARAGE.** Dewitt Brown's Garage was a busy place, dispensing gasoline and fixing flat tires, which were common on the rough mountain roads. (Courtesy of Nannie Greene.)

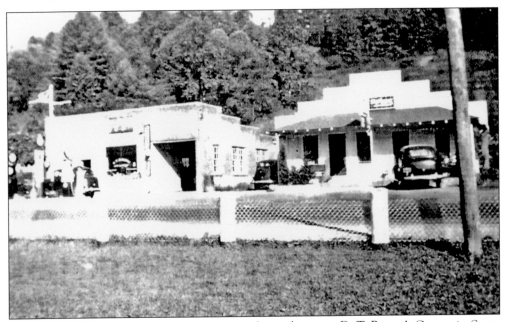

**TOM MOODY'S STORE.** Tom Moody's store was located next to D. T. Brown's Garage in Sugar Grove. It was a community institution for years. (Courtesy of Nannie Greene.)

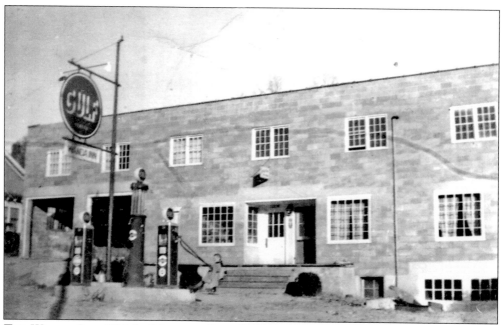

**THE WANDA INN.** This building was Cove Creek's mini-mall. It had a restaurant, store, auto repair station, and gas station, and it also included apartments and rooms for rent upstairs. It was a community gathering place in the 1940s. (Courtesy Nannie Greene.)

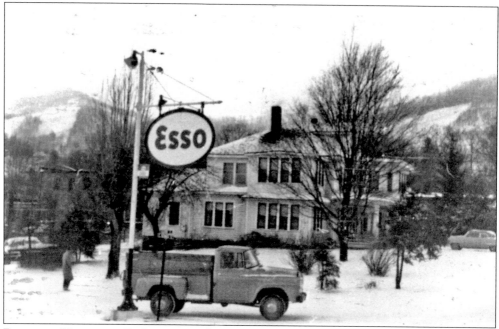

**BINGHAM HOSPITAL.** Built in 1923, this structure served as both a hospital and a home to Dr. Elijah Filmore Bingham. When Dr. Bingham died, his widow, Cordelia Love Bingham, rented rooms to students at Appalachian State Teachers College. In 1959, the property was sold and was converted into the Daniel Boone Inn, a business serving the booming tourism industry. (Courtesy of Historic Boone.)

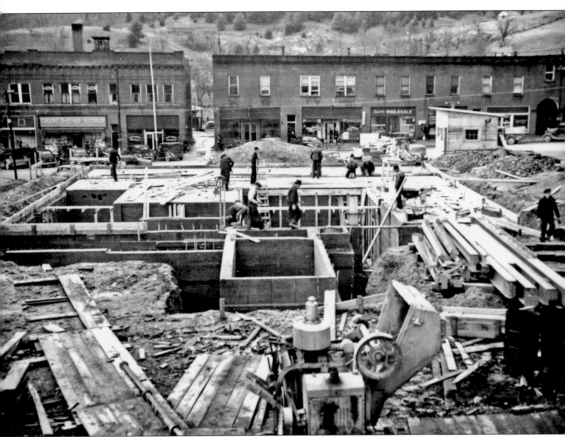

**BOONE POST OFFICE.** Now on the National Register of Historic Places, this photograph shows the 1938 construction of the Boone Post Office. The street that runs in front of the construction site is King Street. The Crest 5-10-25 Store is visible on the left. Just to the right of it is the Boone Post Office that was in use at the time of construction. The construction was a federally funded Works Progress Administration project. An interior wall of the building has a large mural with Boone's namesake, Daniel Boone, as a subject. The town of Boone, which was once called Councill's Store, has had a post office since 1823. The site was previously occupied by the home of J. D. Councill. (Courtesy of Historic Boone.)

**APPALACHIAN THEATRE.**
The photograph at right
shows an unidentified
child standing in front of
the popular Appalachian
Theater in July 1953. The
image below shows the
theater following a winter
storm in late 1941, and *Hold
Back the Dawn* was playing
at the time. In November
1938, the box office was
first opened, and 999 people
could be seated at the then
single-screen cinema. In
the 1970s, the theater was
converted from one screen
to two, so that it could
compete with other newly
constructed theaters in the
area. Later the theater was
known as "the Appalachian
Twin" and also by locals
as "the Dollar Theater."
This theater remained an
important part of downtown
until its closing in 2007.
(Right, courtesy of Brian
Lambeth; below, courtesy of
Richard Trexler.)

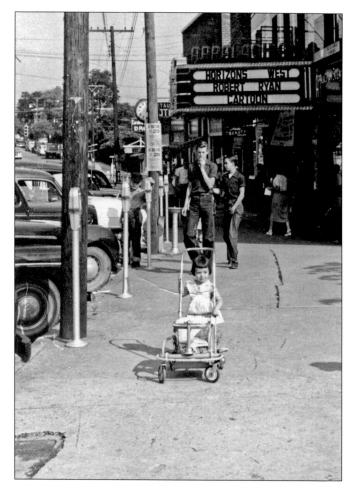

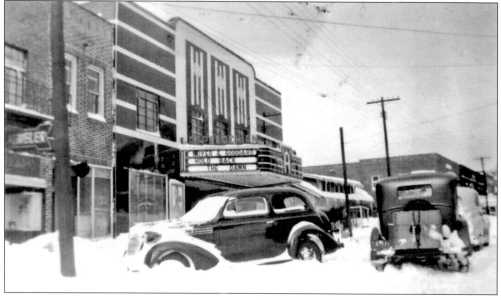

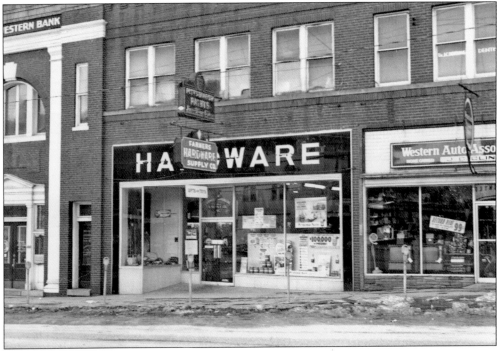

**WEST KING STREET.** The Northwestern Bank, Farmers Hardware, and Western Auto Associate in downtown Boone are photographed in a row in the winter of about 1969. In the 1980s, the Northwestern Bank merged with Wachovia Bank. Then Farmers Hardware expanded into the adjacent property. Note the parking meters, snowmelt along the curb, and the dentist's office on the top right. (Courtesy Historic Boone.)

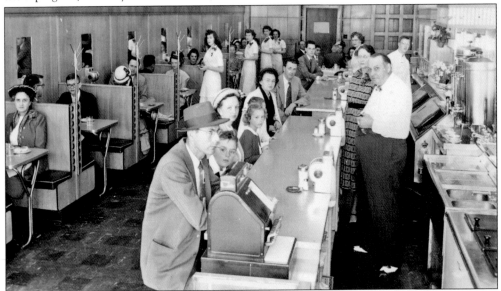

**SKYLINE RESTAURANT.** The Skyline Restaurant was the original meeting place of the Southern Appalachian Historical Association, producers of *Horn in the West*. The restaurant was destroyed by a fire on Christmas Day in 1952. The adjacent Carolina Hotel and City Meat Market shared the same fate. (Courtesy of Brian Lambeth.)

**WATAUGA HOSPITAL.** A nurse and patient are shown outside of the Watauga Hospital in this c. 1942 photograph. Original construction began on the hospital in 1932. Work was suspended for a year due to lack of funds but then resumed in late 1934. The hospital had a 35-bed capacity and served both students and the general public. The hospital now serves Appalachian State University as Founders Hall. (Courtesy of J. P. Greene.)

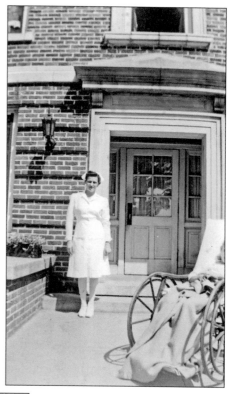

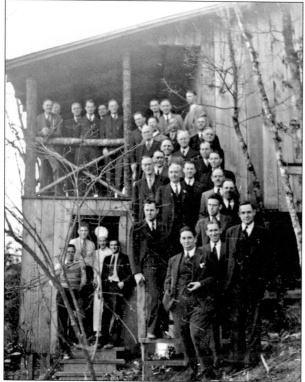

**MILL GATHERING.** Appalachian State Teachers College faculty and staff pose outside of what appears to be the D. B. Dougherty Mill in this c. 1943 photograph. A chef is seen, dressed appropriately, in the lower doorway, perhaps preparing food within. Among those present are business manager Bernard Dougherty (very front), Herbert Wey (top right), and beneath him is D. J. Whitener. (Courtesy of Jane Penley.)

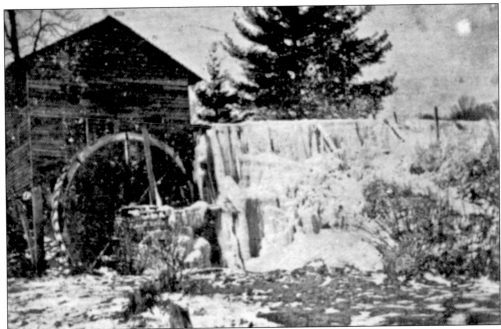

**D. B. DOUGHERTY MILL.** This mill was used to grind food for use in the cafeteria. Food was supplied by farms that were owned and operated by the school. The mill was located near the western side of the present-day CAP Building on Rivers Street. The mill predates the campus and was owned by D. B. Dougherty, father of the Dougherty brothers. This image, originating from a postcard, was produced around 1913. (Courtesy Brian Lambeth.)

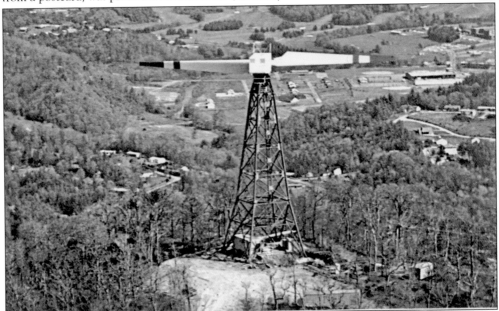

**WINDMILL ON HOWARD'S KNOB.** Construction on this giant wind turbine was completed in May 1979 when the twin 97-foot-long blades were attached. The windmill was part of an experimental program by the U.S. Department of Energy and NASA to research renewable energy. It was situated on the top of Howard's Knob overlooking Boone. (Courtesy of Richard Trexler.)

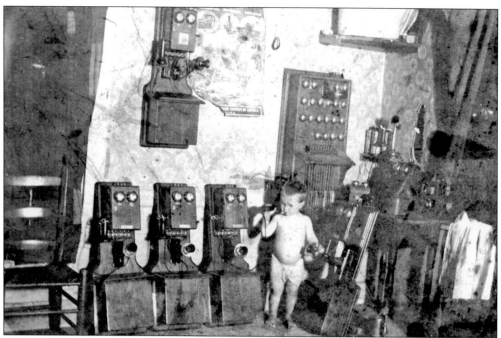

**JACOB MAST.** The headquarters of the Sugar Grove Phone Company was located in the parlor of Pete Mast's store. (Courtesy of Marianna Eggers Isaacs.)

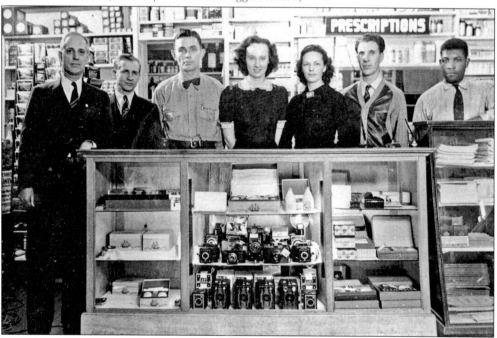

**BOONE DRUG COMPANY.** Dr. George Kelly Moose and John R. McNairy cofounded Boone Drug in 1919. Several doctors rented the space above Boone Drug; constant traffic through the store ensured lasting business. Photographed left to right are Dr. Moose, Pharmacist Wayne Richardson, Bob Agle, Ileen Jones, Delcie Welch, Elijah Bentley, and Haskell Flowers c. 1953. (Courtesy of Watauga Democrat.)

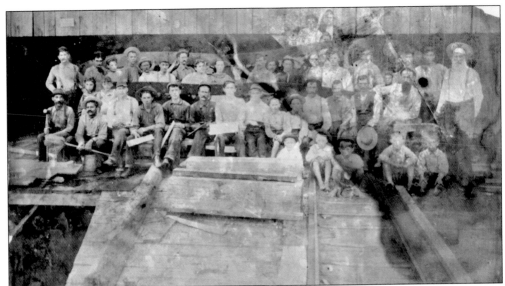

**WATAUGA SAWMILL.** This early-20th-century photograph shows the workers of the Watauga Sawmill. Note the large foot-wide band-saw blade wrapped around the workers. These saw blades, an improvement from the earlier circular saws, were wrapped around two large wheels driven by a steam engine. Wood scraps were used to fire the boiler. (Courtesy of Donna Gayle Akers.)

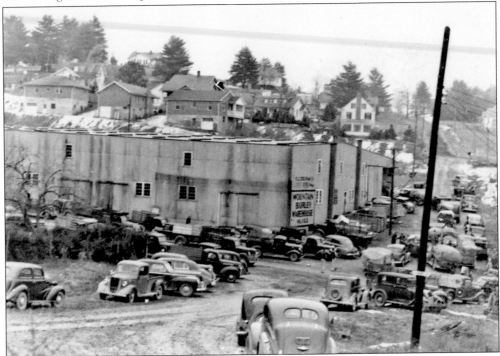

**MOUNTAIN BURLEY WAREHOUSE.** Only six acres of burley tobacco were produced in the county in 1929. By the time this photograph was taken, more than 1,150 acres were growing tobacco. This building was precisely where the present-day Watauga County Public Library now stands. Queen Street is the road going bottom left to top right. The automobiles lend a date of around 1939. (Courtesy of Donna Gayle Akers.)

## Five

# APPALACHIAN STATE UNIVERSITY

**WATAUGA ACADEMY.** Pictured is an advertisement for Watauga Academy taken from the *Watauga Democrat* dated August 9, 1900. Brothers Dauphin D. Dougherty and Blanford B. Dougherty began the school in the fall of 1899 with the goal of providing valuable training for Southern teachers in their profession. Their father, Daniel Baker Dougherty, and their neighbor, J. F. Hardin, donated the land for the school grounds. Supporters donated lumber, labor, and money to aid in the progression of the school's development. The largest monetary gift, $500, came from Moses H. Cone. Between 1899 and 1903, the two brothers erected three cottages, a dormitory for boys, and a dormitory for girls. Records indicate that the first graduating class had 11 students. One hundred twenty-three students attended classes in the spring term of 1903, and the following summer term began with approximately 40 students. The pair did not initially foresee students from outside of the mountains enrolling in classes. (Advertisement by *Watauga Democrat*, courtesy of Brian Lambeth.)

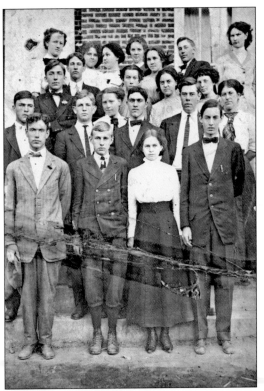

**APPALACHIAN TRAINING SCHOOL.**
Pictured here is the class of 1915 on the steps of the newly constructed science hall. The school had adopted a dress code in 1910 for women that dictated, "Young women are requested to wear inexpensive dresses during the study periods … different classes are urged to organize and to adopt some simple head wear." Maude Lee Farthing (1894–1983) is identified as being second from right in the third row, Maggie Duncan is at the top left, Bill Garvey is in the second row to the right, Blanche Payne is wearing a dress in the first row, and Jeff Stanbury is located to her right. (Courtesy of J. P. Greene.)

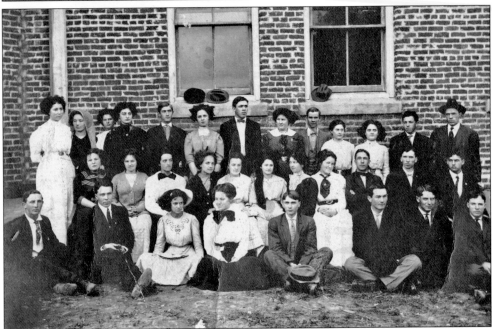

**GLEE CLUB.** The Appalachian Training School had a large auditorium and music rooms on the second floor of the first administration building, which was constructed in 1905. This c. 1915 photograph was taken outside of this building and is perhaps where the Glee Club performed. Carter J. Farthing is identified on the far right of the first row. (Courtesy of J. P. Greene.)

# Students Information Book

—OF—

### Appalachian State Teachers College

BOONE, NORTH CAROLINA

Approved by the Faculty
September First, 1930.

SUGGESTIONS AND RULES FOR STUDENTS OF
APPALACHIAN STATE TEACHERS COLLEGE.

#### GENERAL

1. Students may visit home twice during a semester. They will go by common carrier or by conveyance sent from their homes.
2. Young women are privileged to go up street two times during a week, but not on Sundays or Mondays.
3. No smoking is allowed in Administration building or on campus.
4. Young women are not expected to ride in automobiles, except in going to and from home. They are not expected to stand by an automobile for extended conversation.
5. Every student is expected to join a literary society.
6. Every student is held responsible for damage to property of any kind.

#### DORMITORIES

1. Students in the dormitories are held responsible for any damage to their rooms. No tacks, nails or pins are to be put up in the walls or doors of the rooms. No pictures are to be pasted up in the rooms.
2. Trash should be placed in the receptacles in the halls. Do not sweep up trash in the halls and leave it. ABOVE ALL do not put trash or waste of any kind in commodes.
3. Students are expected to furnish scrubbing powder and soap, and to keep their tubs and basins clean.
4. At the ringing of the bell at 7:00 p. m. students are expected to go to their rooms. When the 7:15 o'clock bell rings every one is expected to be ready to observe study hour.
5. No student is expected to spend the night in town. Students are not expected to be away from town at any time without first seeing the lady in charge of her dormitory.
6. In case of absence, leave in the office of your dormitory your name and the address where you may be found.
7. The school does not furnish medicine for students.
8. Chaperons will be furnished for long trips.
9. No one is expected to carry food from the kitchen, except in case of sickness. Permission must then be secured from the matron of your dormitory.
10. Each student is expected to see that her room is clean, neat and tidy and the light turned off before 8:00 o'clock a. m., except on Sundays, when the hour may be 9:00 o'clock.
11. No electric irons or other heating equipment may be used in the rooms.
12. No student is expected to call out or talk out at the dormitory windows.

#### DINING ROOM

1. All students are expected to be ready and prompt at meals.
2. A warning bell will be given thirty minutes before each meal, except the noon meal.
3. Everyone comes in quietly and stands until the blessing is asked.
4. There should be no loud or boisterous talking or laughing.
5. Everyone is to observe the laws of good etiquette.
6. a. At the ringing of the first bell, the boys retire promptly and quietly.
   b. At the ringing of the second bell, the girls retire promptly and quietly.
   c. No one is expected to leave the dining room until the signal bell rings.
   d. At the ringing of the big bell all young men will leave the campus promptly.
7. No food or equipment of any kind shall be taken from the dining room without permission from the supervisor of the dormitory and the matron of the dining hall, and the equipment thus taken out shall be charged to the person taking it, who shall be held responsible for its prompt return.
8. Young women are not expected to be about the fountain or in front of the Administration building for ten minutes following supper.
9. Students may bring friends to meals provided they secure meal tickets a sufficient length of time ahead so that arrangements can be made.

#### CAMPUS

1. The campus is free to all at given times.
2. When general or special meetings come to a close, the young men will leave the campus promptly — the young women do not attend them on the way.
3. Do not walk on grass so as to make new paths across campus.
4. Students do not drive cars through campus or about dormitories.
5. Students do not collect or stop or loiter on Central Avenue.
6. Young women do not collect on College Avenue or sit on wall along the avenue or on wall along the highway.
7. Steps and walks, leading to Demonstration School, are not places for assembling or visiting.
8. Young women attend those athletic games that are announced at the chapel.

SCHOOL RULES. This partial list of rules may seem impossible to enforce today, but the school administrators of 1930 were convinced that these rules were absolutely necessary. The ideal, published in a separate 1931 bulletin, of the college was to produce teachers "of vigorous health, high mentality, broad and thorough scholarship, high professional spirit, genuine skill in the art of teaching culture in the amenities of life, pleasing personality, and sterling character." Grades were measured by a letter scale from "A" to "F." This scale included the letter "E," which represented "a passing type of work," and the letter "F" represented a failure. The college employed 30 faculty members, enrolled a student body of 800 during the regular terms, and a student body of more than 1,300 during the summer term. (Courtesy of Brian Lambeth.)

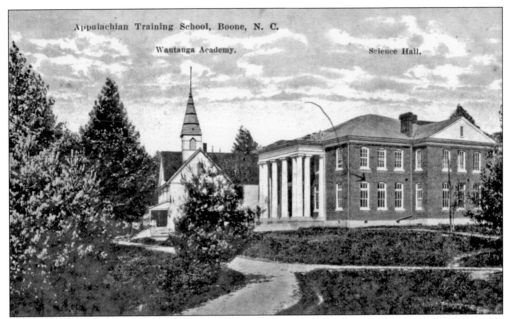

**CAMPUS, C. 1912.** The building known as Watauga Academy (left) was built in 1899 by the people of Watauga County and countless other benefactors. The seemingly small, two-story structure was used to teach art on the first floor and housed a library, a printing office, a sewing room, and an archive on the second floor. The Science Hall (right) was constructed in 1911. The building had a basement and two floors that housed laboratories, a museum, an auditorium, men's society halls, and recitation rooms. (Courtesy of Brian Lambeth.)

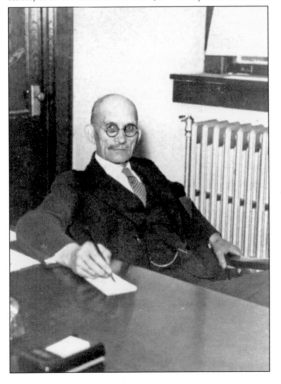

**B. B. DOUGHERTY.** Seated is the eminent Blanford Barnard Dougherty, B.S., Ph.B, D.Lit., D.Ed. Both he and his brother Dauphin were responsible for the creation of what is now Appalachian State University. Blanford was president for the school's first 56 years, during which time, he never drew a salary for himself. "A child's opportunity for education in North Carolina should not depend upon being born in close proximity of wealth," is a quote from Dr. Dougherty. He briefly continued with the title of president emeritus for two years until his passing in 1957. (Courtesy of Brian Lambeth.)

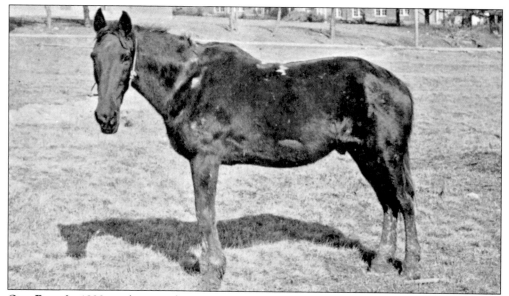

**OLD BOB.** In 1899, at the age of one, Old Bob was placed in the service of Watauga Academy and the public schools of Watauga County. B. B. Dougherty was the county superintendent of the public schools in Watauga, and it was his task to visit each school periodically. Dougherty and Old Bob traveled together in each of these visits during a period of 16 years. Old Bob then spent the rest of his life on the school campus in various small roles. Old Bob was said to have extraordinary intelligence. At the age of 30, Old Bob died and was interred on the school campus, complete with an engraved stone marker. (Courtesy of Brian Lambeth.)

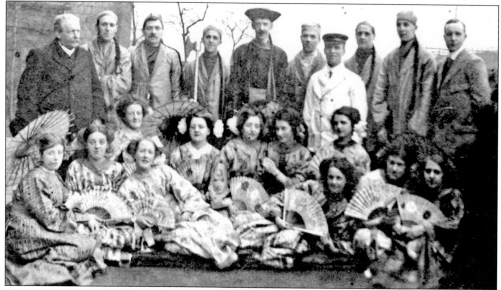

**CHINA DAY.** History professor D. J. Whitener is identified as standing in the second row at far left. No documentation is provided with this unusual 1933 photograph of students dressed in native Chinese attire. At the time, only American and European history courses were taught. Chinese sentiment at this time was poor; many federal laws prohibited immigration and marriage of Chinese. With prejudices aroused nationwide, this image captures a celebration of diversity rather than a mockery. (Courtesy of Brian Lambeth.)

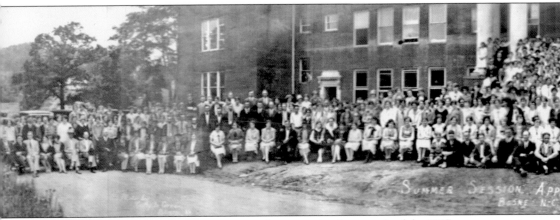

**STUDENT BODY.** Pictured is a commissioned panoramic photograph of the 1927 summer session of the Appalachian State Normal School. The photograph is dated June 23, 1927. The almost three-year-old administration building serves as the backdrop for exactly 582 students and faculty

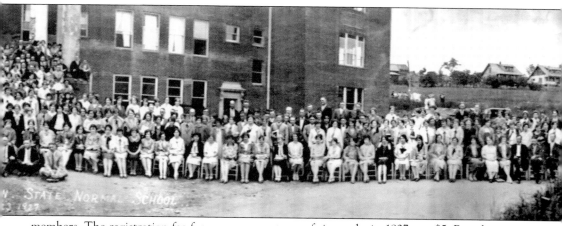

members. The registration fee for one summer term of six weeks in 1927 was $5. Boarding in a campus dormitory for those six weeks cost $27. (Courtesy of Brian Lambeth.)

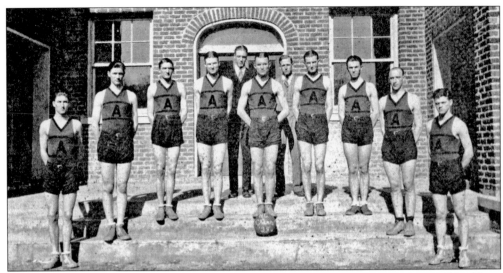

**BASKETBALL.** This 1928 photograph was taken outside of the area's first Justice Hall building. Coach C. B. Johnston is standing in the center of the second row. From left to right are Fitzhugh Hurley, Grant Donnelly, Russell Hodges, Frank Chappell, C. B. Johnston, and Walter Sullivan. The remaining players are not identified. The following basketball season of 1929–1930 yielded 14 wins to 5 losses against college teams in the state. Rivals included Guilford College, Catawba College, and Lenoir Rhyne. The basketball on the steps reads, "N.C. Champs '28." (Courtesy of Historic Boone.)

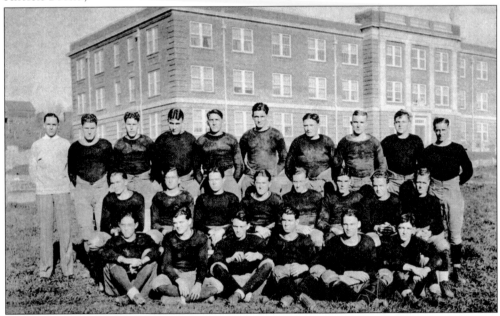

**FOOTBALL.** Pictured here is the 1929–1930 Appalachian State Teachers College football team with the girls' dormitory in the background. This season marked the second year of Mountaineer football. Four victories, one loss, and three scoreless tie games were recorded. Pictured wearing white on the far left is the team manager, ? Lipscomb. On the far right in the third row is coach C. B. Johnston, and directly in front of him is assistant coach G. P. Eggers. (Courtesy of Historic Boone.)

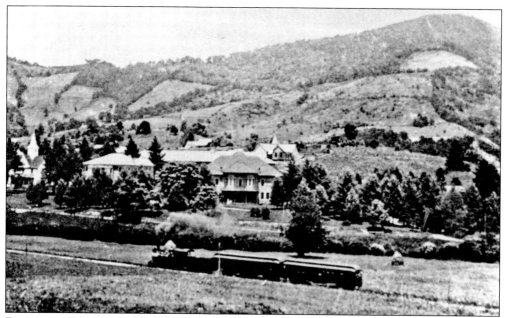

**RAILROAD TERMINUS.** An ET&WNC locomotive, known by locals as *Tweetsie*, is seen here steaming away from campus around 1925. The train ran a route to Boone until the 1940 flood destroyed much of its tracks in Watauga County. The first administration building, constructed in 1905, is seen in the center. The Science Hall and Watauga Academy with its steeple are visible to the left. Howard's Knob is the mountain peak in the background. The Depot Street of today is named for the station and tracks that once existed. Boone was the eastern terminus of this railway, and Johnson City, Tennessee, was the western terminus. (Courtesy of Historic Boone.)

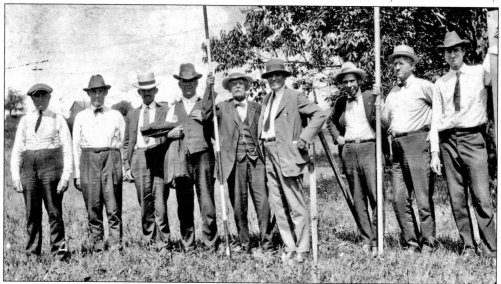

**GROUND-BREAKING.** The activity pictured here, about 1922, is most likely either the surveying for or the running of power lines for a new building. The men are identified from left to right as ? Lorn, ? Allen, B. B. Dougherty, E. S. Coffey, E. F. Lovill, ? Blair, and three unidentified. Coffey and Lovill served on the board of trustees at the time, along with T. C. Bowie, Adolphus Taylor, J. M. Barnhardt, M. B. Blackburn, and E. F. Watson. (Courtesy Historic Boone.)

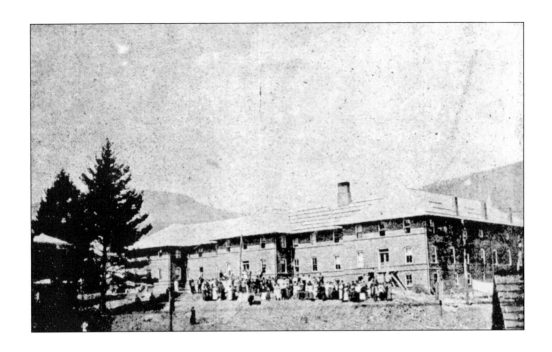

**OUT WITH THE OLD.** Pictured twice is the same building, the New Dormitory for Girls. At the time of its destruction, it was called the Lovill Home. The structure was erected in 1915 and had 75 dormitory rooms, society halls, a kitchen, and a dining hall that could seat 300. After Dr. W. H. Plemmons was installed as president in 1956, many construction projects commenced. Plemmons intentionally held meetings with budget commissions in some of the more run-down buildings on campus so that they might see the conditions firsthand. The New Dormitory was razed in 1967 so that Sanford Hall could be built. (Courtesy of Brian Lambeth.)

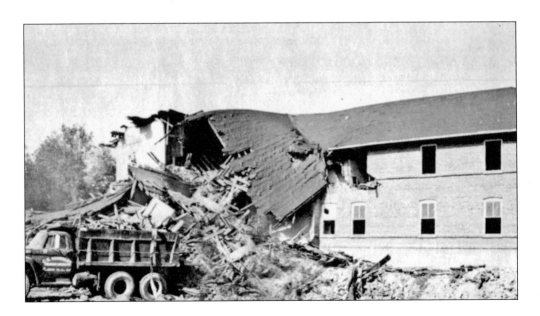

KEEPING IN TOUCH. The first *Dew Drop* hit mailboxes in 1900. This informal newsletter served as a source for news, events, and photographs of the school. The length and frequency of the pamphlet varied between the years of 1900 and 1930. Editions were bound by glue, string, or staples, and were mailed in matching open-end envelopes. The larger annual "catalogue" editions contained the entire course offerings. The June 1921 *Dew Drop* pictured here is bound by black and gold string. (Courtesy of Brian Lambeth.)

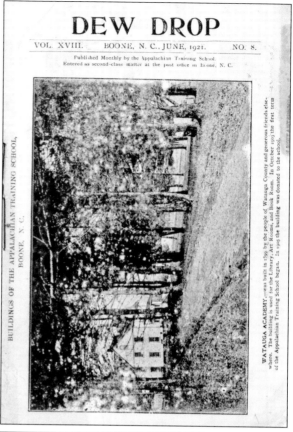

# DEW DROP

VOL. XVIII.          BOONE, N. C., JUNE, 1921.          NO. 8.

Published Monthly by the Appalachian Training School.
Entered as second-class matter at the post office in Boone, N. C.

BUILDINGS OF THE APPALACHIAN TRAINING SCHOOL, BOONE, N. C.

WATAUGA ACADEMY.—was built in 1899 by the people of Watauga County and generous friends elsewhere. The building is used for the Library, Art Rooms, and Book Room. In October 1903 the first term of the Appalachian Training School began. In 1905 the building was donated to the school.

# THE APPALACHIAN

Published Bi-Weekly by the Students of Appalachian State Teachers College

VOLUME I—NUMBER 1          BOONE, NORTH CAROLINA, OCTOBER 9, 1934          PRICE 10c PER COPY

## OVER 500 EXPECTED FOR HOMECOMING

\* \* \* \*   \* \* \* \*   \* \* \* \*   \* \* \* \*   \* \* \* \*   \* \* \* \*   \* \* \* \*

## New College Library to Be Completed By Christmas

### New Structure Will Hold 60,000 Books

Dr. Dougherty Says Work on Hospital Building Will Be Resumed at Once; Completion of New Gymnasium Marks High Point in Physical Education Standard.

The new library building will be completed and 60,000 volumes moved into it by the Christmas holidays, it was announced this week by Dr. B. B.

### Grid Battle And Playcrafters Feature Elaborate Program

More than five hundred former students will converge upon the campus of Appalachian State Teachers College Saturday to attend the annual Homecoming Day festivities.

The feature of the program for Homecoming Day will be the grid battle between Appalachian's Moun-

ni; responses from the alumni (George Sudderth presiding); reading or special music; announcements; closing song, "Alma Mater," students.

II. 11:30. Open house for visiting in all departments; 12:00, plate lunch in Central Dining Hall (optional). Proceeds will be used to

### Three New Faculty Members Added

Miss Hall, Miss Liles and Professor Grubbs Come to Appalachian College for Year of 1934; Grubbs and Miss Hall Are Completing Work on Ph. D. Degrees.

Three new members have been added to the college faculty this year.

Miss Carrie Hall, in the English department; Miss Leila Liles, in the De-partment; Miss Leila Liles, in the De-

CAMPUS NEWSPAPER. The *Appalachian* became the school's student-published newspaper in 1934. Pictured here is the title mast of the first issue, dated October 9, 1934, and was priced at 10¢. Dozens of area merchants advertised in the paper. The editor's note in this issue stated that no staff has been selected and that the issue is largely an experiment to gauge demand. The *Appalachian* is still being published today. (Courtesy of Brian Lambeth.)

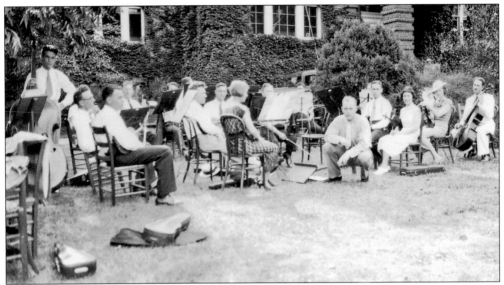

**OUTDOOR PERFORMANCE.** The partial symphony orchestra of the Appalachian State Teachers College is pictured here at an outdoor performance. The school's symphony orchestra was first featured in the 1949 campus yearbook, the *Rhododendron*. This *c.* 1955 photograph shows double bassist Barry Ruth standing on the far left. (Courtesy of Historic Boone.)

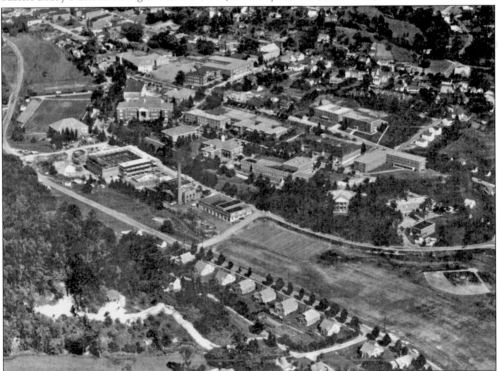

**CAMPUS AERIAL, 1955.** Today's Rivers Street begins in the lower right corner and is lined with faculty housing and trees. Broome-Kirk Gym (middle left and left of steam plant) is seen under construction. Tennis courts to the right of the steam plant are under construction as well. Today's East Hall and Founders Hall are pictured in the middle right. (Courtesy Historic Boone.)

# *Six*

# FRIENDS AND NEIGHBORS

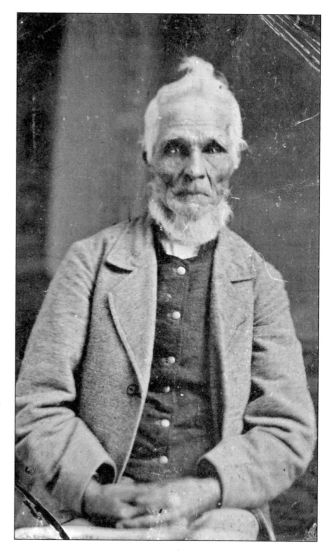

**DUDLEY FARTHING (1804–1895).** Born in Henrico County, Virginia, Farthing is shown in this tintype. His father, William Watkins Farthing (1782–1827), was a missionary in Watauga County, eventually moving his family to Beaverdam in 1826. Dudley became a prosperous farmer and was the first judge of Common Pleas and Quarter Sessions in Watauga County in 1849, holding the first session in a sheep barn, where all in attendance were harassed by fleas left by the former occupants. He and his wife, Nancy Mast, had 13 children. William W. and his brother John sold out in Wake County shortly after the death of their father and moved to Beaverdam with 23 children (some young adults) between them. (Courtesy of J. P. Greene.)

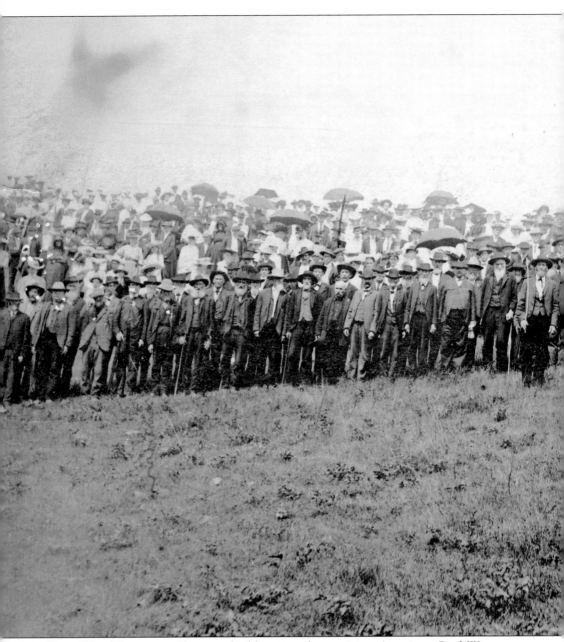

**CIVIL WAR VETERANS.** Photographed here are the surviving American Civil War veterans from Watauga County about 1910. An incursion of Union troops began on March 28, 1865, and brought the conflict directly to Watauga County. The troops, under command of Gen. George Stoneman, approached Boone and came under fire from a house where the Boone Post Office now

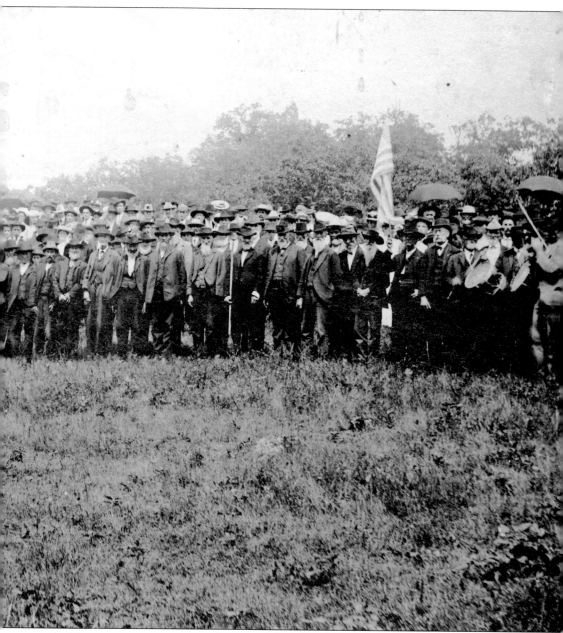

stands. The men were organized as a home guard for Boone. Stoneman's troops returned fire and drove the group of men toward Howard's Knob. Most of those men were shot from behind while escaping; three men were killed. The skirmish ended, and the troops made their way to Blowing Rock and Deep Gap before heading east to Wilkes County. (Courtesy of J. P. Greene.)

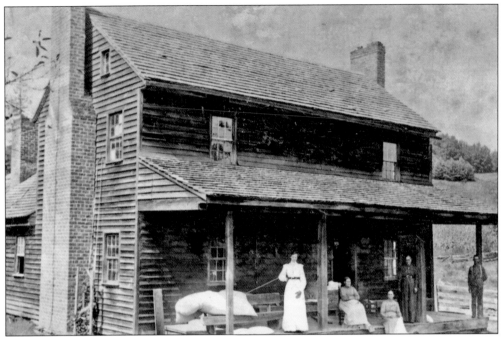

DUDLEY FARTHING HOUSE, C. 1905. This *c.* 1850 home was built in the Bethel Community. On the porch are (from left to right) Hattie Greer Greene (1882–1977), Susan Farthing (1833–1922), Emiline Farthing (1852–1917), Sarah Farthing Greene (1849– 1932), and Dudley F. Greene (1879–1957). The house was one of the first in the county built of sawn boards and survived until 1952. (Photograph by James C. Shell, courtesy of J. P. Greene.)

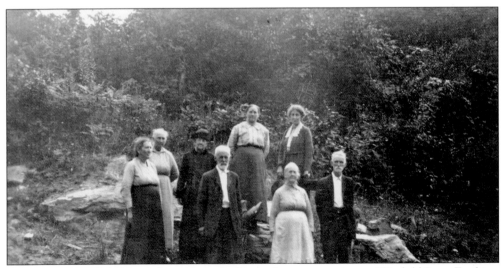

FARTHINGS, C. 1910. Pictured outside in the Beaverdam community are Winfield Scott Farthing (1848–1928, left), a teacher, and J. Elbert Farthing (1854–1948, right), a farmer. Before publicly funded schools reached rural areas, teachers were hired, or subscribed to, by groups of parents. Winfield Farthing taught several subscription schools in Watauga County and Johnson County, Tennessee, to the west. The others in the photograph are unidentified. (Photograph by James C. Shell, courtesy of J. P. Greene.)

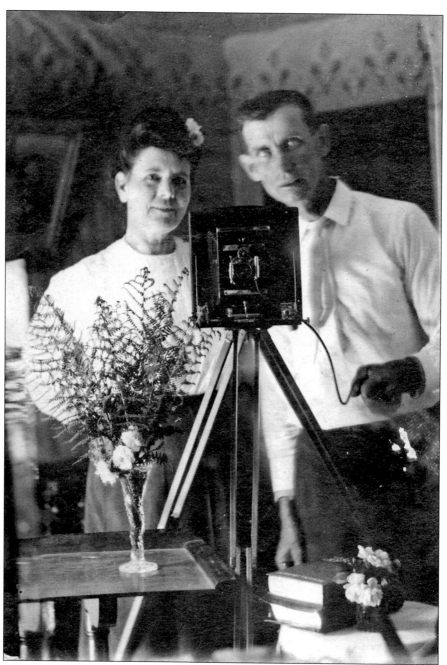

**JAMES AND CALLIE SHELL.** This is a self-portrait of James C. Shell (1864–1937) and his wife, Calista (Callie) Thompson Greer Shell (1863–1942), in their home in Beaverdam about 1900. From their appearance, this was likely one of Shell's first shots. James was a storekeeper, cabinetmaker, photographer, and farmer in the Beaverdam area. Callie made dresses and bedspreads for sale, shipping some of her spreads to Baltimore. In 1932, they relocated to Banner Elk, where they became houseparents at the Grandfather Home for Children, and James taught woodworking at Lees McRae. Their daughter, Crathy Shell Guy, became a noted regional artist. (Photograph by James C. Shell, courtesy of J. P. Greene.)

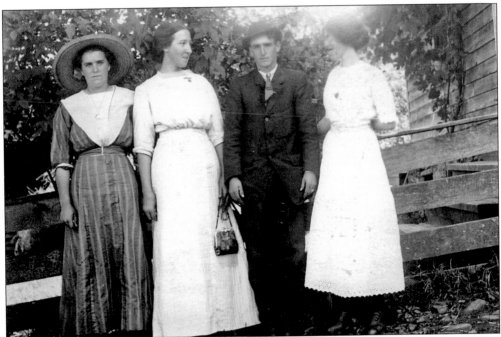

**WEDDING.** From left to right are Ida Melinda Ragan Johnson, Hettie Green Ragan, Robert Soloman Ragan, and Ivel Lawrence on April 15, 1914. Hettie and Robert (center) are the bride and groom. (Courtesy of Jane Penley.)

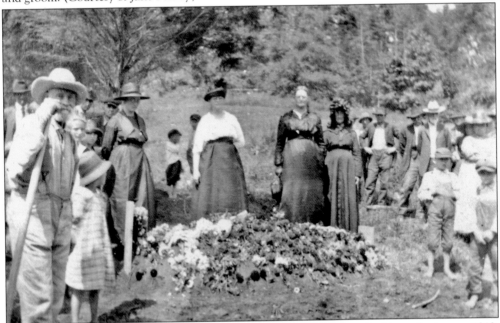

**FUNERAL.** The burial of Mary E. Farthing (1888–1912) was photographed in early August 1912. Behind the grave are her aunts Susan Farthing (1833–1922) in white blouse and Sarah (Sally) Farthing Greene Cable (1849–1932) in black holding hat, and her mother Emiline Farthing (1852–1917) in a bonnet. The location of the cemetery is on the Dudley Farthing Farm on John Shell Road in Bethel. (Photographed by James C. Shell, courtesy of J. P. Greene.)

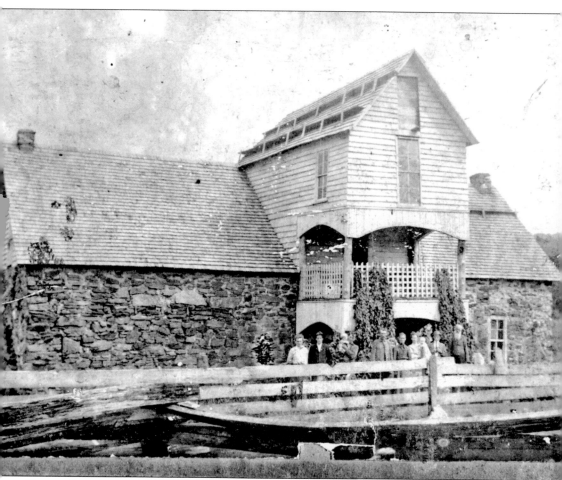

**RAGAN FAMILY, 1915.** Photographed here is the Rock House in the Rich Mountain community. The building was constructed in 1850. The occupants of the house at this time were the Ragan family. Billy Ragan, his wife, Susan, their children, and other family members are shown here. The house was situated on the O. M. Little Farm. Fire devastated much of the original structure and left only the original rock walls. A portion of the original structure was used as the foundation and frame of another building, which still stands today. (Courtesy of Jane Penley.)

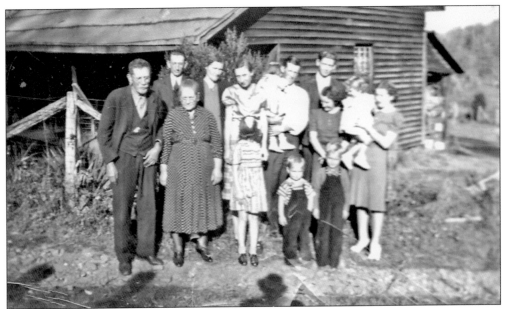

**COBBS CREEK.** From left to right are (first row) Alfred Brown; his wife, Melissa Trivette Brown; ? Hodges; Joe Franklin Greene; Nancy Elizabeth Greene; and Bunnie Edith Hodges holding Shelly Ann Carroll; (second row) Tom Vannoy; Maude Hodges Vannoy; Lois Carroll; Rhonda Carroll; Lewis Hodges; and unidentified. They are at the old home place on Cobbs Creek, which is no longer standing. (Courtesy of Warren Greene.)

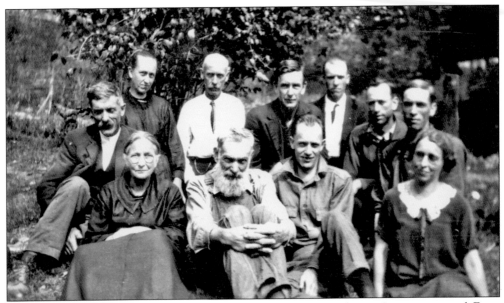

**GREENE FAMILY, C. 1910.** The family of Mary and Jacob Greene of Meat Camp is pictured. From left to right are (first row) Mary Elizabeth Gragg Greene; her husband, Jacob Harrison Greene; Horton Greene; and Mary Epsie Greene; (second row) Calvin Columbus Greene; Neilie Greene Poe; Wesley Greene; Benjamin Bergin Greene; Johnson Greene; Richard Alfred Greene; and Wiley Greene. Wesley Greene was a local musician who played banjo at local community gatherings. (Courtesy of Warren Greene.)

**ELIJAH J. NORRIS.** Confederate veteran Elijah J. Norris, son of Ephriam and Margaret Greene Norris, is standing with sword in hand. Note the artificial backdrop and the ground visible in the front of the photograph. (Courtesy of Faye Greene.)

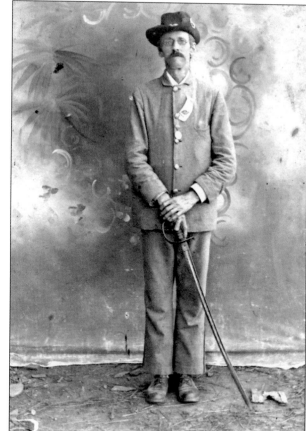

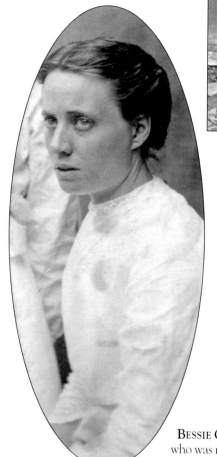

**BESSIE GREENE.** Sitting pretty is Bessie Melinda Barnes Greene, who was married to Benjamin Greene and lived in the Meat Camp community. (Courtesy of Warren Greene.)

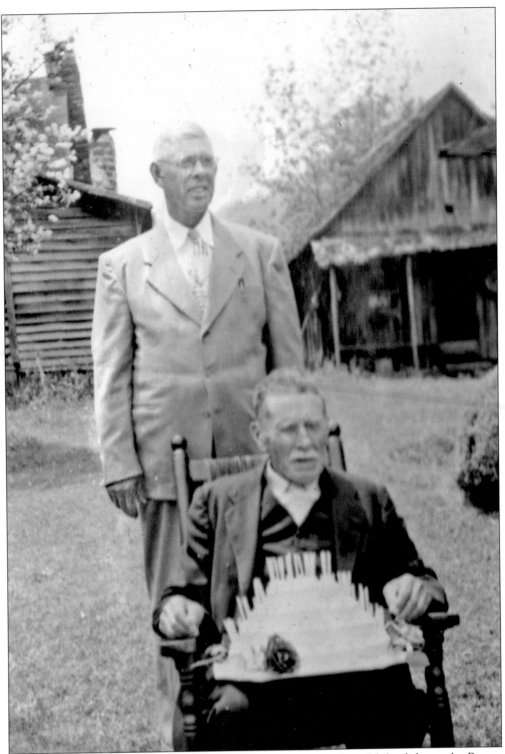

**Eggers Birthday.** Shown is preacher Roby Eggers (seated) on his 95th birthday at the Brown homeplace on Cobbs Creek Road. (Courtesy of Warren Greene.)

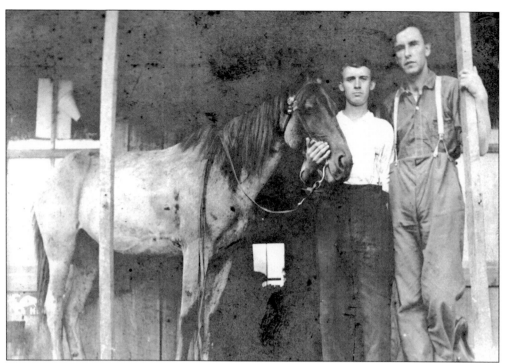

**GOING TO TOWN.** Lloyd Norris (left) and Ben Greene are posed with a horse in front of an old store in the Meat Camp area. (Courtesy Warren Greene.)

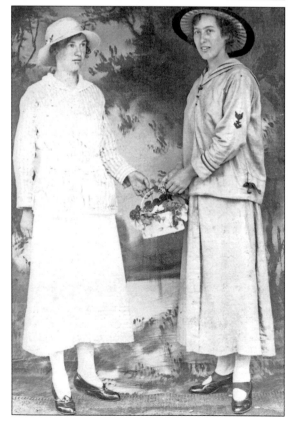

**LOVELY LADIES.** Posed in front of a photographer's backdrop are two lovely young ladies. Susie Hagaman (1898–1957) who later married A. E. Trivette, is standing on the right dressed in a stylish nautical outfit. She was a teacher for several years at one-room schoolhouses such as Rominger and Ivey Ridge. The identity of the lady on the left is unknown. (Courtesy Ned Trivette.)

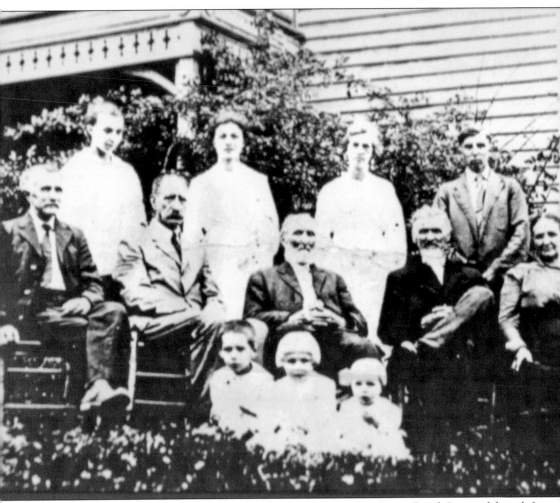

**GREENE FAMILY.** The Greenes are sitting outside their house on Peoria Road. Pictured from left to right are (first row) Fred Tester, Susie Tester, and Ruth Tester; (second row) Henry Greene, unidentified, Adam Greene, and two unidentified; (third row) Una Greene Tester, Clara Greene Farthing, Janie Greene Dishman, and Robert Greene. The individuals in the third row were all Henry Greene's children. (Courtesy Ned Trivette.)

**Mr. and Mrs. A. E. Trivette.** Audie "A. E." Eldridge Trivette (1892–1970) and his wife, Susie Hagaman Trivette (1898–1957), pose in front of the lovely Greene homeplace on Peoria Road c. 1940. A. E. was a farmer who sometimes drove turkeys to market in Butler, Tennessee, and who operated a small country store near the house. Their son Ned Trivette has restored the house and lovingly cares for it today. (Courtesy Ned Trivette.)

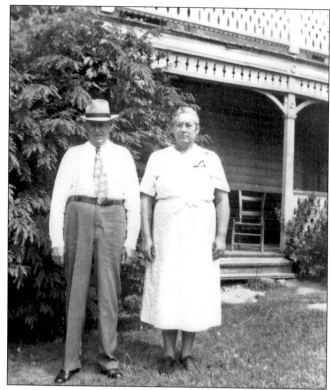

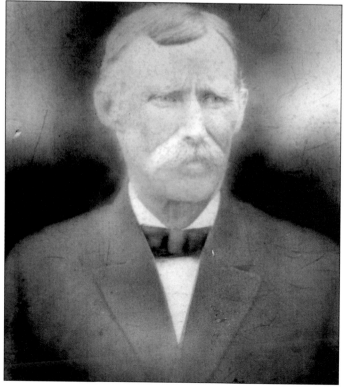

**Solomon Trivette.** Solomon was a farmer in the Rush Branch area. His father, Wilburn Trivett, was killed by bushwhackers during the Civil War. (Courtesy of Ned Trivette.)

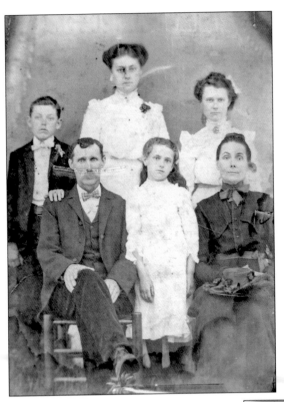

**SOLOMON TRIVETTE FAMILY.** From left to right are (first row) Solomon Trivette; Trusty; and Jane Billings Trivette; (second row) A. E., Verdie, and Mallice. The family is dressed in the latest styles of the day, complete with bow ties, hats, and brooches. (Courtesy Ned Trivette.)

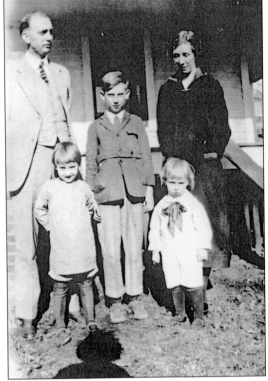

**S. C. EGGERS SR. FAMILY.** Taken about 1926–1927, this photograph of the S. C. Eggers Sr. family includes, from left to right, S. C. Eggers, Christine, Emsley, Stacy Clyde Jr., and his wife, Nora South Eggers. S. C. Eggers Sr. was involved in the real estate business. Sadly, Emsley was killed in World War II. Christine was a housewife. Stacy founded a family law firm in downtown Boone, which he still works in today. (Courtesy of Stacy Eggers Jr. and Margaret Eggers.)

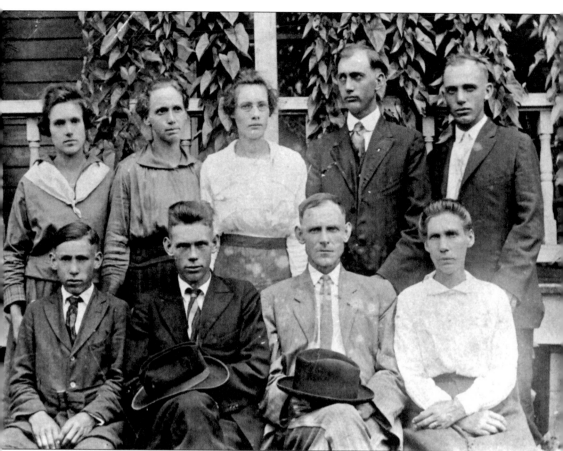

**EMSLEY ROBERT EGGERS FAMILY, C. 1920.** Emsley Robert Eggers is pictured here with his wife and grown children. From left to right are (first row) Floyd Paul Eggers, Harrison Clay Eggers, Emsley Robert Eggers, and his wife, Lucinda Matilda Johnson Eggers; (second row) Mae Eggers Robinson, Bessie Eggers May, Alice Eggers Isaacs, Stacy Clyde Eggers Sr., and Donley Hill Eggers. Emsley and his family lived in the Beaverdam area, and he was the sheriff of Watauga County about 1912–1913. (Courtesy Stacy Eggers Jr. and Margaret Eggers.)

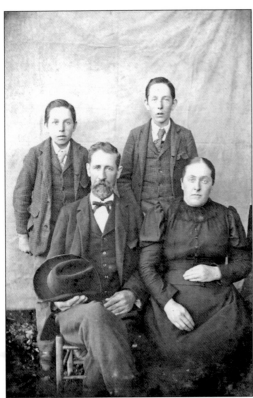

**SOUTH FAMILY.** Pictured from left to right are (first row) Ike Lundy and Sally Lundy; (second row) David South and Grover South. (Courtesy Margaret Eggers.)

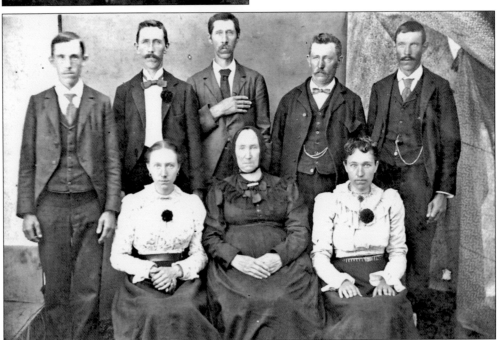

**SOUTH FAMILY.** The following members of the South family are, from left to right, (first row) Roselle, Polly, and Samantha; (second row) Frank, Henry, Jim, Enoch, and George South. (Courtesy Margaret Eggers.)

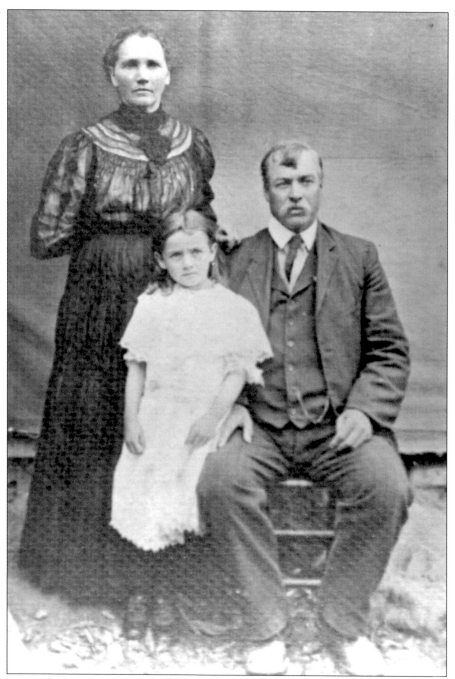

**Dr. Bingham and Family.** Cordelia Love Bingham (standing on left), their child Ruth, and Dr. Elijah Filmore Bingham are posed in this photograph. Dr. Bingham was the first man from Watauga County to graduate from medical school and practice in Watauga County. A doctor in the Cove Creek area, Bingham walked and rode on horseback to the most remote areas to treat the sick. W. R. Lovill, a Boone attorney, said of Bingham, "say whatever you please about him, you can never overdraw his character." Dr. Bingham also owned the Bingham Roller Mills in the Cove Creek area. (Courtesy of Margaret Eggers.)

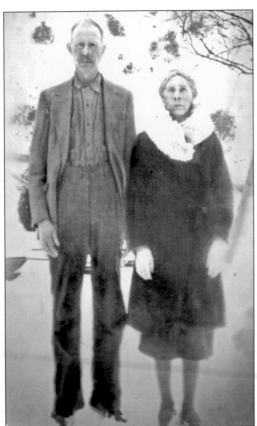

**McGuires.** William Richard McGuire and Lucy Louartie Wright McGuire are shown in this photograph taken in the Matney community. William was a farmer and also did construction on Highway 194. They are relatives of Wilbur and Orville Wright. (Courtesy of Glenda Baird Vance.)

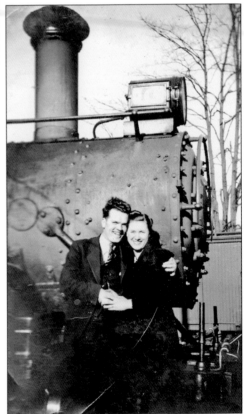

**ET&WNC Engine.** Bob Forrester and Anna Lee Norris are posed next to an ET&WNC train engine in the wintertime. (Courtesy of Warren Greene.)

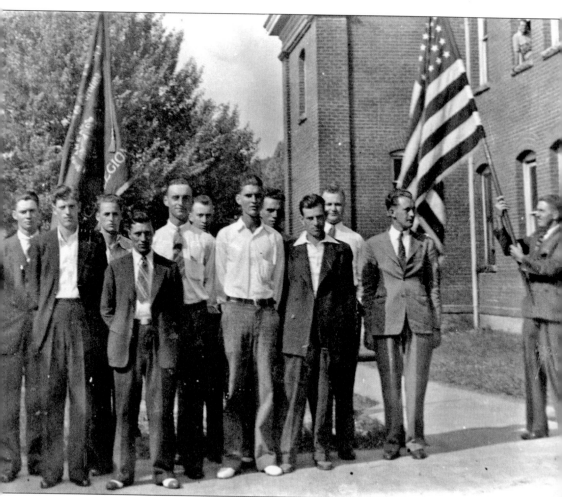

**WORLD WAR II DRAFTEES.** Watauga County draftees of World War II are pictured outside of the courthouse on June 21, 1941. Among those identified are Buster Wilson of Beaverdam (second from left), Byumn Dancy of Zionville (third from left), James L. Penley of Rich Mountain (fifth from left), and Laferene Fox of Boone (eleventh from left). Eighty-eight men from Watauga County were sent into action on June 30, 1941. Of the 2,200 draftees from the county, 63 were lost. The entire population of the county was 18,000 in 1940. (Courtesy of Jane Penley.)

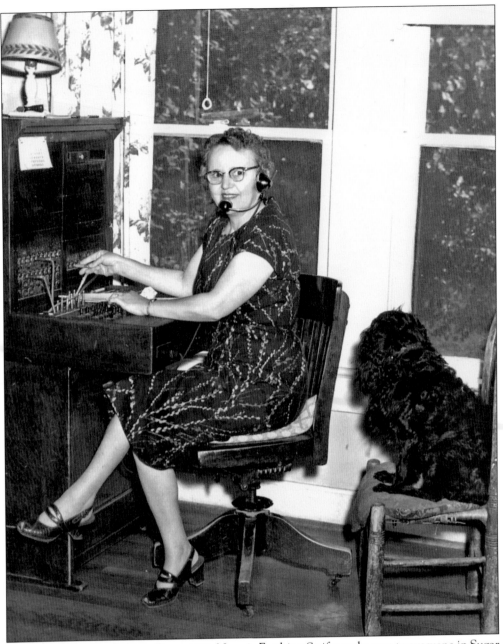

**NANNIE SWIFT, TELEPHONE OPERATOR.** Nannie Farthing Swift was known to everyone in Sugar Grove because she was the voice on the telephone system. She was the operator for the party-line system from the early 1940s until it was sold to Skyline Telephone in 1954. The first telephone system in the county started in 1907. (Courtesy Nannie Greene.)

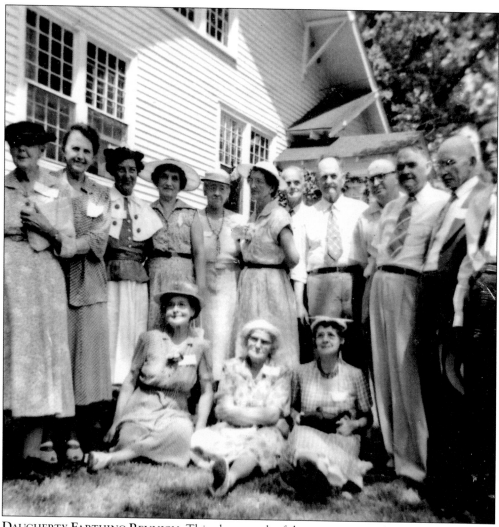

**DAUGHERTY-FARTHING REUNION.** This photograph of the reunion was taken in 1952 in Boone. B. B. Dougherty is second from the right, and Carter J. Farthing is fourth from the right. (Courtesy of J. P. Greene.)

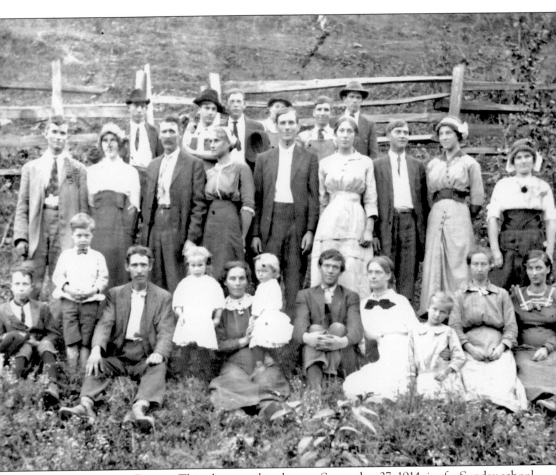

**SUNDAY SCHOOL PICNIC.** This photograph, taken on September 27, 1914, is of a Sunday school class from Windie Gap Church, now the Zion Hill Church. These folks have on their "Sunday best" clothing. A few of them are identified as follows: (first row) Albert Trivette (third from left); Albert's father, Drew Trivette (fourth from left); an unidentified Trivette child (fifth from left); Drew's wife, Lizzie Trivette (sixth from left); and another unidentified Trivette (seventh from left); (second row) fifth from the left Edward Boone Hagaman (fifth from left); and his wife, Susie Belva Hagaman (sixth from left). (Courtesy of Ned Trivette.)

**COURTIN'.** Palmer Sligh Blair and Sarah Lynn Rives are on a date in their courting days. They were married on October 25, 1947. Palmer Blair, the foremost photographer in the area, operated Palmer's Studio in downtown Boone until his passing in March 1957. Sarah, with an incidental knowledge of photography and some hired photographers, took over operations for the next nine months until the shop was sold to George Flowers in 1958. (Courtesy of Sarah Lynn Blair Spencer.)

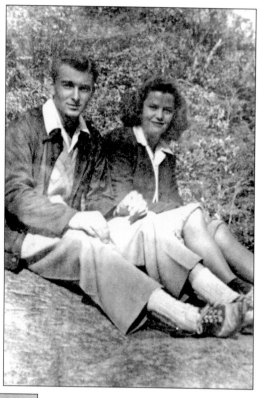

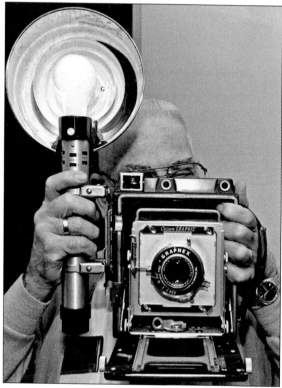

**GEORGE FLOWERS.** In 1958, George Flowers opened Flowers Photo Shop in what was once Palmer's Studio in downtown Boone. Originally from Hickory, he and his wife, Millie, fell in love with the community and decided to make Boone their home for the rest of their lives. Flowers was a photographer for United Press International from 1944 to 1992 and operated a photography shop in Boone until the late 1990s. (Courtesy of Historic Boone.)

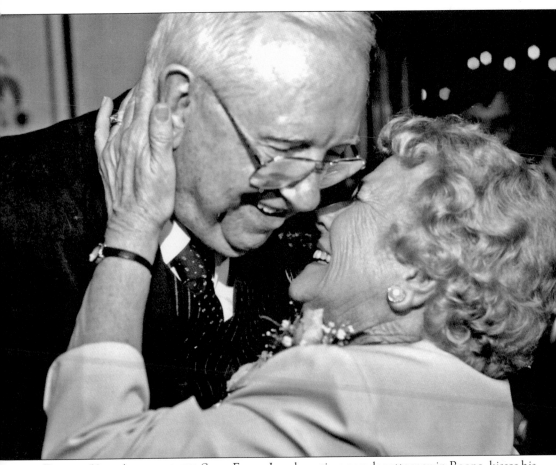

**EGGERS 50TH ANNIVERSARY.** Stacy Eggers Jr., a long-time popular attorney in Boone, kisses his wife fondly at their 50th anniversary party. (Courtesy of Becca Eggers-Gryder.)

# Seven

# RECREATION AND TOURISM

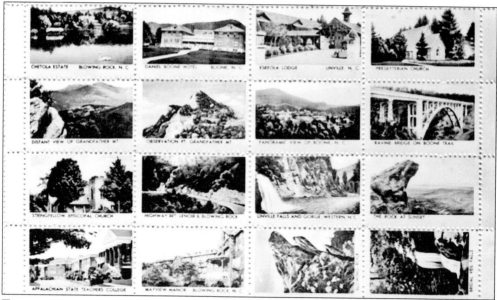

TOURISM MEMORABILIA. This small plate of 16 collectible stamps features scenes of Blowing Rock, Boone, and the Linville areas of North Carolina. As tourism continued to grow, the demand for memorabilia and printed advertisements increased. Postcards, photographs, brochures, and other items were in high demand as visitors wanted a pleasant reminder of their travels here. Many of the larger shops in the towns of Watauga County carried a wide selection of camera and film equipment. These stamps were produced by the Asheville Postcard Company in 1934 and gave the recipient views of the biggest area attractions of the time. The selection includes places to stay, places to worship, what roads to take, and what landmarks could be found on the way. Memorabilia from this time period is highly collectible today. (Courtesy of Brian Lambeth.)

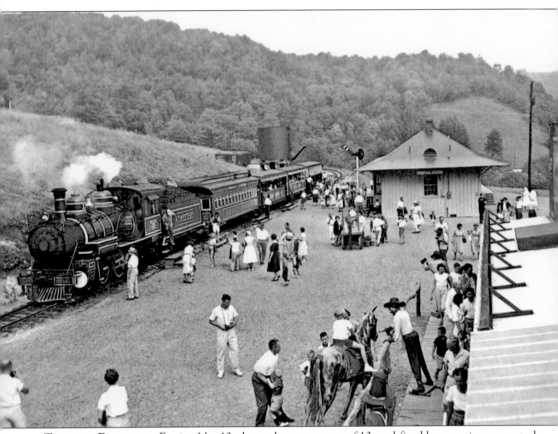

**TWEETSIE RAILROAD.** Engine No. 12, shown here, was one of 13 coal-fired locomotives operated by the ET&WNC and dates back to the late 1800s. The railroad operated originally from Johnson City, Tennessee, to Cranberry, North Carolina. By 1917, the railway reached Watauga County and would later lead directly to Boone from Cranberry. The flood in August 1940 devastated most of the track built in Watauga County, and those portions were never repaired. *Tweetsie* continued service to Cranberry until 1950. After changing hands a few times, once to performer Gene Autry, and finding itself in Virginia, *Tweetsie* began its journey back on May 20th, 1956. North Carolina governor Luther M. Hodges officially declared that day be "*Tweetsie* Homecoming Day." The train was moved by rail to Hickory, North Carolina, and restored over a period of one year. On May 23, 1957, *Tweetsie* arrived in the county, where it continues to operate today. This 1958 postcard shows *Tweetsie* and its passenger cars freshly installed at the railroad attraction. (Courtesy of Brian Lambeth.)

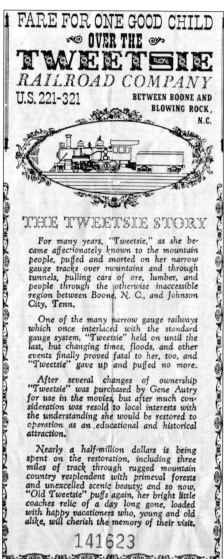

TWEETSIE RAILROAD CHILD'S TICKET. The appeal and popularity of frontier living to the youth in the 1950s and 1960s drew crowds of children to the railroad. Around this time, characters such as Daniel Boone and Davey Crockett were portrayed on television, movies, and comic books in grand adventures, sometimes even involving Native Americans. Parents were fans of both the entertainment and the educational aspects the attraction provided to their children. With a 1957 origination, several generations of locals and tourists have handed down their enjoyment of this unique amusement park to their children and grandchildren. The *Tweetsie* Railroad continues to feature elaborate dramatizations, beautiful scenery, and relics of ages passed along the track's course around Roundhouse Mountain. (Both, courtesy of Brian Lambeth.)

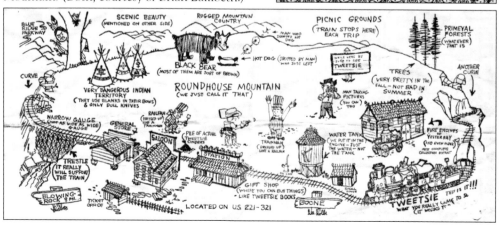

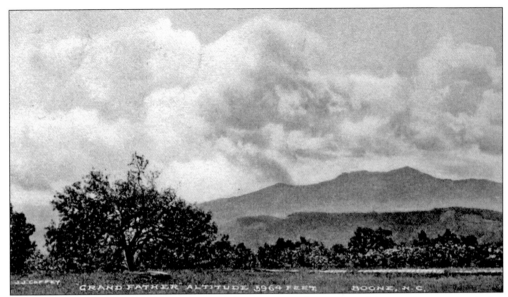

**GRANDFATHER MOUNTAIN.** This postcard demonstrates the topographic prominence, or relative height, of Grandfather Mountain to the surrounding area. Grandfather Mountain rises 2,444 feet above the surrounding landscape and captures large areas of the horizon in the southern sections of Watauga County. This card is postmarked 1910, making it one of the earliest examples of commercially produced postcards from the area. (Courtesy of Brian Lambeth.)

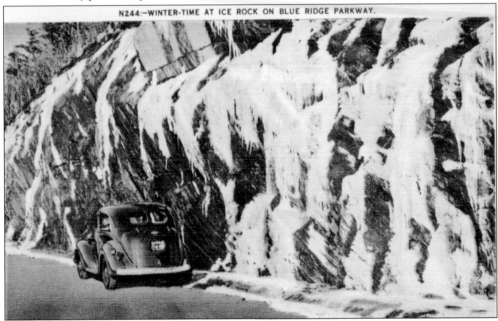

**ICE ROCK.** This postcard was produced in 1946 by the Asheville Postcard Company. After World War II, construction was continued on the Blue Ridge Parkway, and the tourism machine turned back on. The reverse side reads, "Ice Rock, on the Blue Ridge Parkway, is so called because it has an icy appearance throughout the year. Much of the time in the summer it is covered with water, which in the light resembles ice, and during the greater part of the winter the water stays frozen on its surface." (Courtesy of Brian Lambeth.)

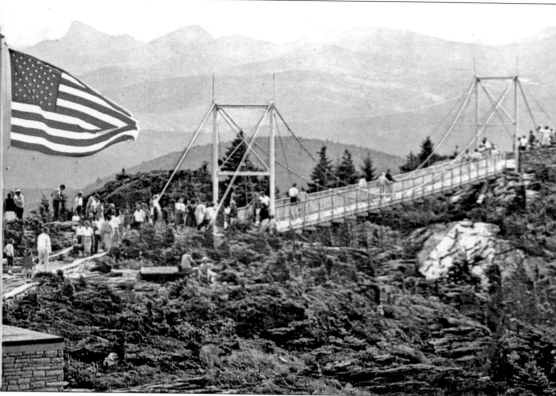

**MILE-HIGH SWINGING BRIDGE.** Walking across this 228-foot-long bridge has always been a popular tourist activity since its opening. Appropriately, the North Carolina tourism director gave the bridge this name during the dedication ceremony in 1952. The expanse sits 5,305 feet above sea level, taking it 25 feet beyond a mile in elevation. It is a suspension bridge that, by nature, sways and is not rigidly constructed. The bridge crosses over an 80-foot chasm beneath the Linville Peak of the mountain. Charles Kuralt made note of these measurements in 1992 and said, "It is calculated that six million people have come up here to see the Mile-High Swinging Bridge. How many of them would have made the trip if it were advertised as the 80-foot-high swinging bridge?" The views from the bridge and surrounding beauty have made this bridge a required destination for any visitor. (Courtesy of Brian Lambeth.)

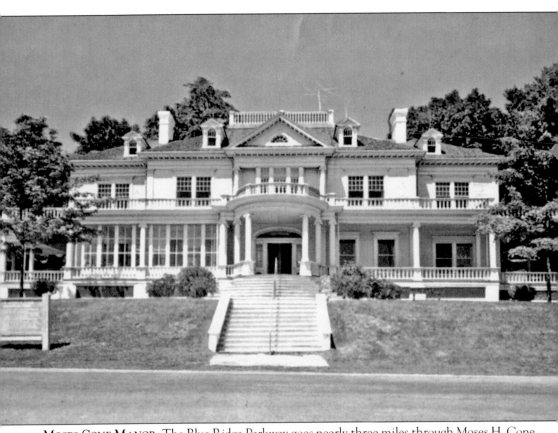

**MOSES CONE MANOR.** The Blue Ridge Parkway goes nearly three miles through Moses H. Cone Memorial Park. The centerpiece of the park is Moses Cone Manor, also known as Flat Top Manor, due to its proximity to Flat Top Mountain. This Colonial Revival manor was built around 1901 by Moses Cone, a successful textile entrepreneur. Moses and his wife, Bertha, purchased more than 3,500 acres of land to place the manor on. On the grounds, Moses demonstrated many newly developed methods of agriculture. Apple orchards, gardens, livestock, and fish lakes were maintained with the labor of approximately 30 tenant farmers and their families, who lived on the estate grounds. The manor is now home to a craft center. The park is open all year and features walking trails, horseback riding, and fishing lakes. (Courtesy of Brian Lambeth.)

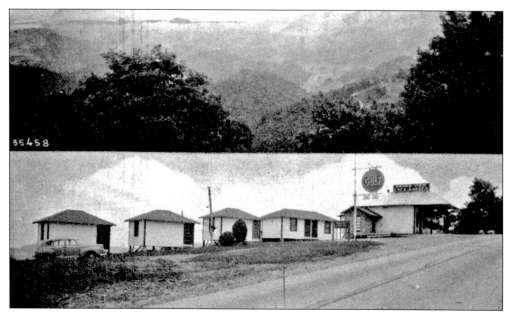

**BLUE RIDGE PARKWAY TOURISM.** The construction of the Blue Ridge Parkway through the county created many businesses that accommodated tourists. Pictured here is a two-pane postcard showing "Grand View" cabins and an overlook. The car is a 1941 Buick. Around the same time, construction of the parkway was put on hold as the labor force departed for war duty. The reverse side reads, "Beauty Beyond Belief, Modern Cabins. Mr. and Mrs. Grant Greene, Owners. US 421, Deep Gap, NC." (Courtesy Brian Lambeth)

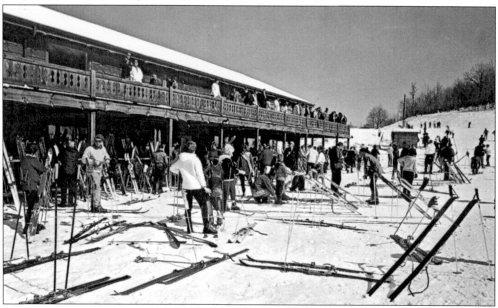

**BLOWING ROCK SKI LODGE.** This ski lodge, under the direction of M. E. Thalheimer, first opened as a corporation for the 1962–1963 winter ski season. The business had early success, but the operation had debilitating financial trouble. The corporation was sold and renamed to Appalachian Ski Mountain in the 1968–1969 season. At that time, there were only rope tows and no chairlifts. (Courtesy of Brian Lambeth.)

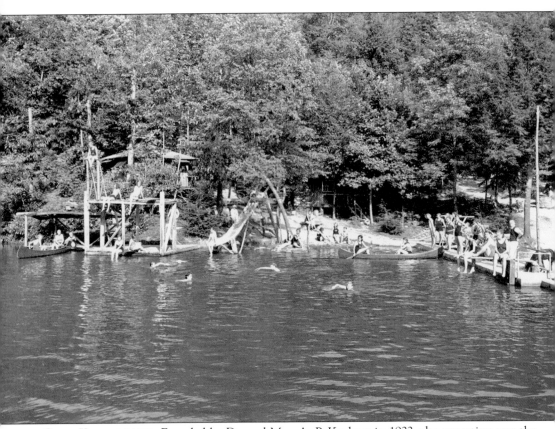

**CAMP YONAHLOSSEE.** Founded by Dr. and Mrs. A. P. Kephart in 1922, the operation was the first girls' camp in North Carolina. Affluent girls would come to the camp to swim, horseback ride, and create various crafts. The lake in this 1931 photograph is artificial and was created by a wooden dam. Watauga County is home to few natural lakes. (Courtesy of Richard Trexler.)

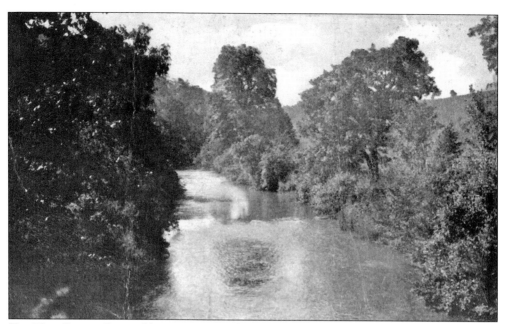

**THE NEW RIVER.** Pictured here is a postcard of the New River as it appears near Boone, North Carolina. The New River flows to the north and eventually into the Ohio River. The many species of game fish available in these waters attract many sports fishermen. This card was postmarked in 1923. (Courtesy of Brian Lambeth.)

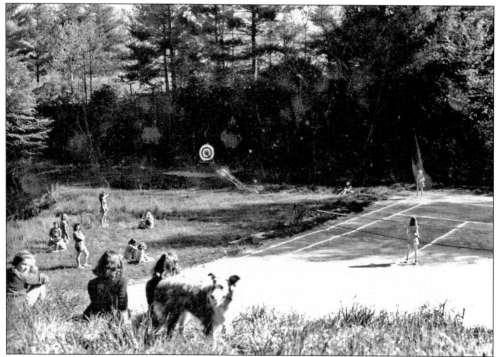

**SPORTING GIRLS.** These girls from the Valle Crucis School for Girls are enjoying tennis and archery. These sports would have been practiced at schools and camps within the area. (Courtesy Valle Crucis Conference Center.)

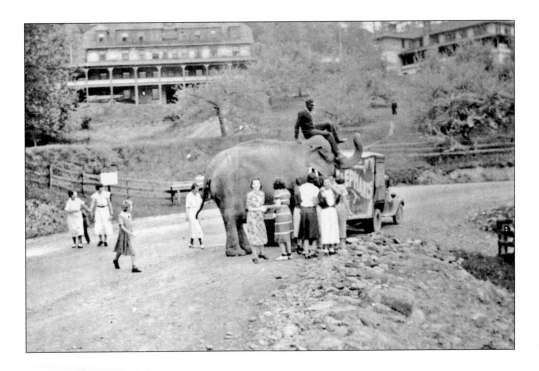

CIRCUS IN VALLE CRUCIS. In the c. 1935 photograph above, a truck is loaded with a car for elephants on a visit to Valle Crucis. In the past, small circuses traveled across the country by train or truck and set up shows in many small towns. The girls of the Valle Crucis School are amazed at the size of this elephant from the Haag Circus. The elephant trainer appears to be African American, which is unusual for the time period. (Both, courtesy of Valle Crucis Conference Center.)

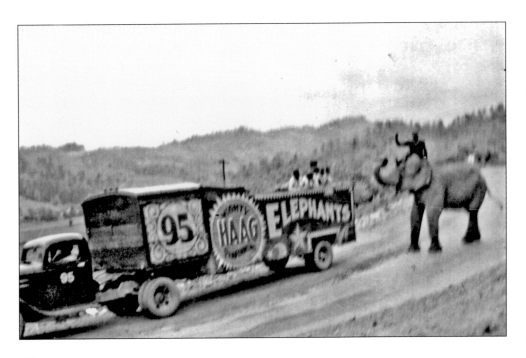

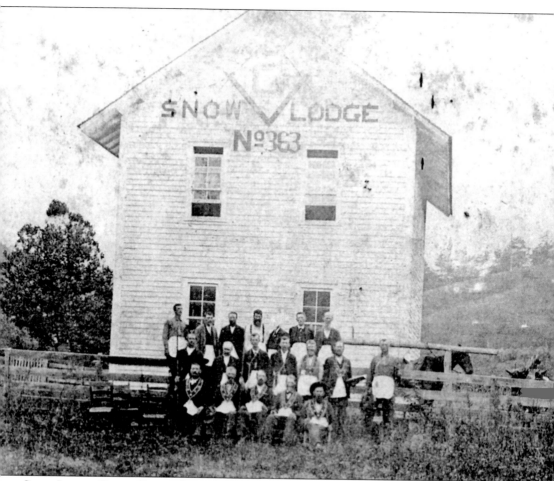

**SNOW LODGE.** Pictured here is Snow Lodge, a meeting place for Masons, the Eastern Star Shriners, and the Scottish-Rite groups. The man seated in the first row on the right, wearing the brimmed hat, is likely the master of the lodge. Hats were worn to signify rank and status. The man standing behind the master of the lodge appears to be holding a Great Light of Masonry, likely the Bible (the Torah, Bible, Quran, and other religious holy books are considered Great Lights of Masonry). In the second row, two gentlemen are holding staffs, the emblems of the senior and junior deacons. The building was later sold and is now a rental property. (Courtesy of Nannie Greene.)

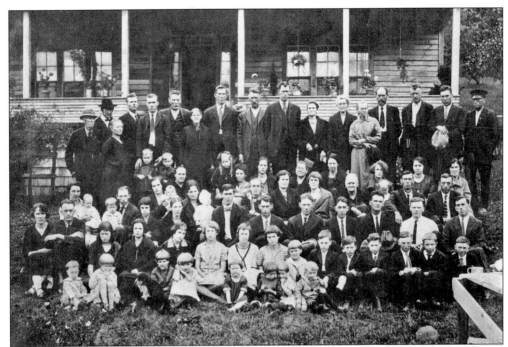

**WEDDING.** The wedding of Nannie ? and Nathan M. Greene is pictured here. Both were from the Meat Camp area. (Courtesy of Warren Greene.)

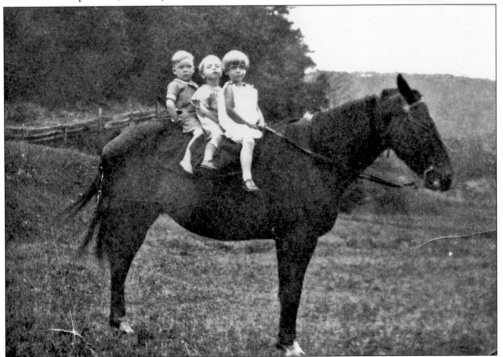

**GREENE COUSINS HORSEBACK RIDING.** Riding "Old Charlie" are (from left to right) Con Greene, Polly Greene, and Patty Greene of the Meat Camp community. Horses were dependable transportation in this mountain geography. (Courtesy of Warren Greene.)

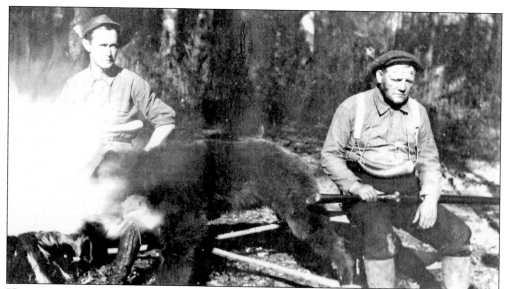

**HUNTING BEAR.** Two members of the Coffee family are posed holding their rifles and their prized trophy, a small American black bear, around 1920. A 2004 count by the State of North Carolina determined that a population of 11,000 black bears inhabits the state. (Courtesy of Historic Boone.)

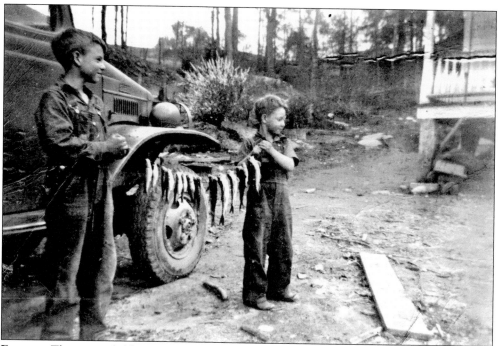

**FISHING.** These two children are proudly displaying their string of fish caught from the Watauga River in the late 1940s. Their catch appears to have several larger channel catfish on the right and small-mouth bass on the left. The Watauga River is also home to rainbow, brook, and brown trout, and attracts many sports fisherman. (Courtesy of J. P. Greene.)

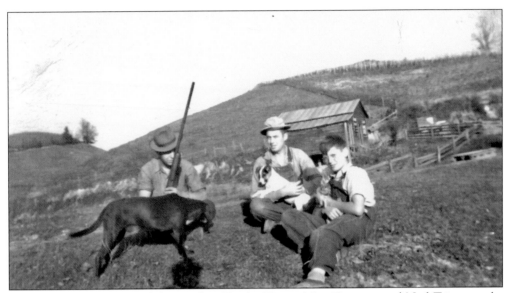

**RABBIT HUNTING.** From left to right, Charles Tester, Max Trivette, and Ned Trivette take a break from rabbit hunting on the Trivette farm. Hunting is still a favorite recreational activity in this rural area. The Trivette's Cash Grocery Store is standing in the background. (Courtesy Ned Trivette.)

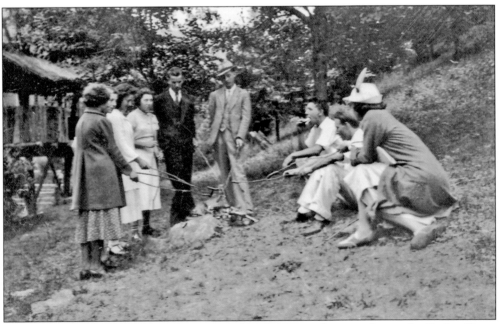

**CAMPFIRE COOKING.** This group is roasting hot dogs around a campfire in the Poplar Grove area. (Courtesy of Warren Greene.)

**PICNIC AT THE RIVER.** Clyde A. Tester and Mary Faye Trivette Tester stand on a large rock beside Elk River in this *c.* 1948 photograph. Picnics, walks, and hikes along local waterways and trails continue to be popular pastimes. (Courtesy of Ned Trivette.)

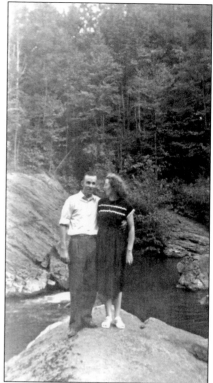

**SHAPE-NOTE SINGING.** This dapper group (pictured below) of young ladies and men are studying their songbooks at a shape-note singing school. These gatherings were held during the summer and often lasted an entire week. The two ladies in the back seem to be holding a banner. (Courtesy of Ned Trivette.)

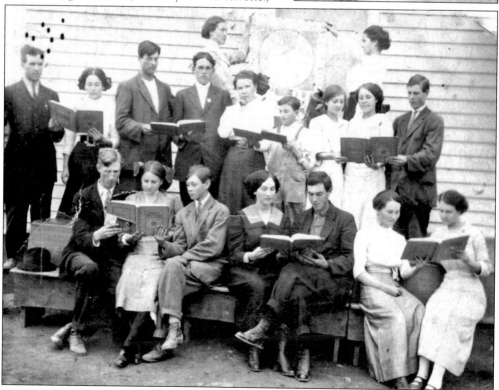

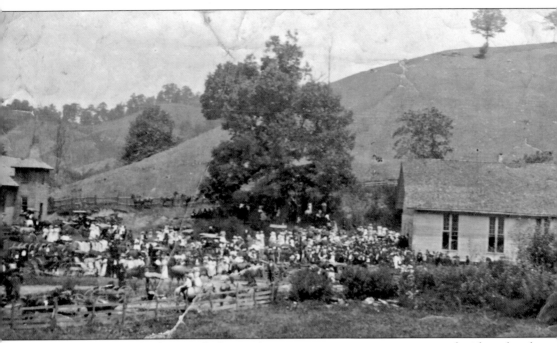

**BAPTISM.** This early photograph shows a baptism service at a spring or stream beside a church somewhere in the county. Baptisms were social events, with dinner on the grounds usually following the joyous event. (Courtesy of Ned Trivette)

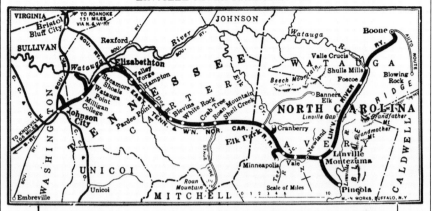

**The Rhododendron**

**EAST TENN. & WESTERN NORTH CAROLINA RAILROAD CO.
LINVILLE RIVER RAILROAD CO.**

## Spend Your Vacation In The Mountains

Now is the time to make your plans for the summer outing.

These lines, popularly known as "The Narrow Gauge," pierce the most attractive vacation grounds in the Southeast.

This railroad extending from Johnson City, Tennessee, to Boone, North Carolina, covers the greatest variety of natural scenery east of the Rockies, within so short a distance.

The section of Western North Carolina served by the "Narrow Gauge" affords all the attractiveness of the ideal vacation land; altitude, climate, rugged mountains, virgin forests, and beautiful streams where trout abound.       •

For further information and descriptive literature, call on or address,

### GENERAL PASSENGER DEPARTMENT

EAST TENNESSEE & WESTERN NORTH CAROLINA RAILROAD CO.

JOHNSON CITY,  :  :  :  :  :  :  TENNESSEE

**ET&WNC Railroad Map.** This route map of the Eastern Tennessee and Western North Carolina Railroad was published in a 1920s *Rhododendron* yearbook by the Appalachian Training School. The Linville River Railroad had its terminus in Boone (top right). Students and visitors coming from areas to the west of Boone had this narrow-gauge line, a railroad with rails about 3 feet apart, to convey them. From the south, the method of travel would have likely been by railroad to Lenoir and then to Boone by automobile. From the east and other parts of North Carolina, railway would have been used to North Wilkesboro, and a bus or jitney service would carry them to Boone over the roadways. (Courtesy of Brian Lambeth.)

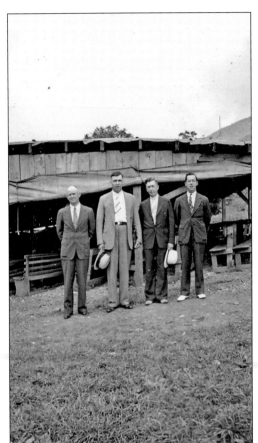

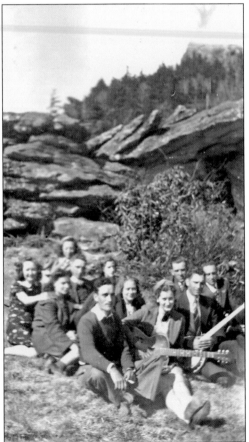

**REVIVAL.** Tabernacle revivals were held in this frame shed, which was located across from the Watauga County courthouse at the later location of Smithy's Department Store in Boone. (Courtesy of Warren Greene.)

**CHURCH PICNIC.** This Meat Camp Baptist Church Sunday school is having a picnic at Grandfather Mountain. From left to right are (first row) John Greene, Bunnie Edith Hodges holding a guitar, and Alex Wilson with the banjo. (Courtesy of Warren Greene.)

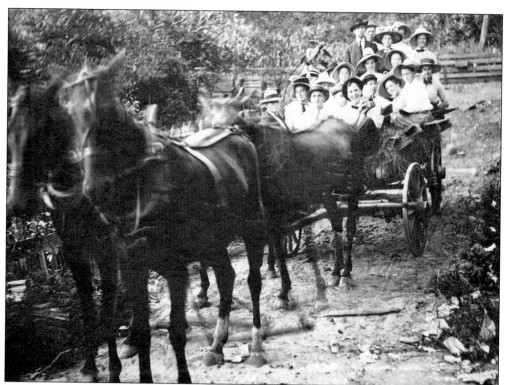

**SUNDAY OUTING, C. 1920.** A horse-drawn wagon is carrying a group of children during a Sunday outing in the Bethel area. The two individuals who are identified are James Brown Farthing (far left), and Carter Joseph Farthing (holding a fruit jar). The fruit jar was most likely filled with water. James became a farmer and storekeeper. Carter became the superintendent of the state prison camp in Boone in the 1940s and 1950s and was active in church work. (Courtesy of J. P. Greene.)

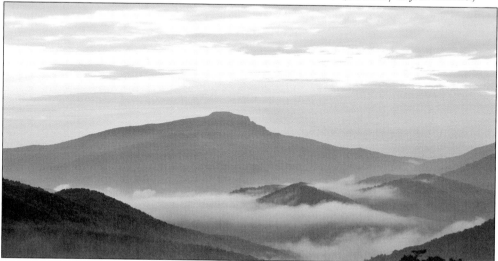

**THE FACE OF GRANDFATHER MOUNTAIN.** The name of Grandfather Mountain is derived from the perception of a face in the contours of its top. This peak is highly recognizable in the county due to its elevation of 5,964 feet. This particular view is available when traveling from the east or north toward Grandfather Mountain. (Courtesy of Wayne Sumner.)

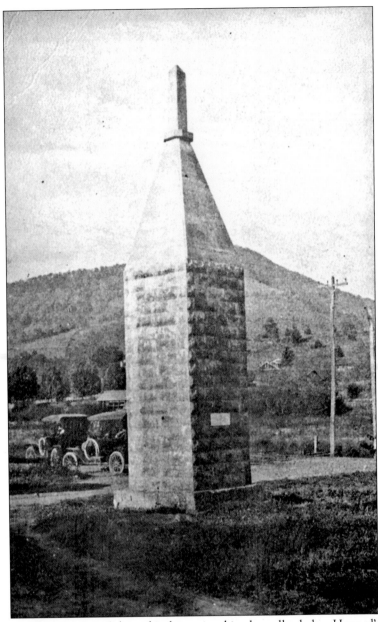

**DANIEL BOONE MONUMENT.** A log cabin has existed in the valley below Howard's Knob since around 1750. It is said that hunters and trailblazers used the cabin when they found themselves in the area. The most famous tenant was Daniel Boone. Up until 1911, the chimney stones of this cabin were still in their original foundation and served as a lingering memorial of Daniel Boone. Col. William Lewis Bryan, the first mayor of Boone, saw a need for a more permanent and lasting memorial to honor his distant relative, Daniel Boone. In 1911, Col. W. L. Bryan started the monument without assistance from anyone; he was 74 at the time. In the fall of 1912, the monument was completed with no unveiling and no fanfare. In the late 1960s, the monument was razed due to the construction of a new road. It was not until 2005 that a replica of this obelisk would materialize. The replica now stands, with pieces of the original incorporated, at the corner of Depot and Rivers Streets. (Courtesy of Brian Lambeth.)

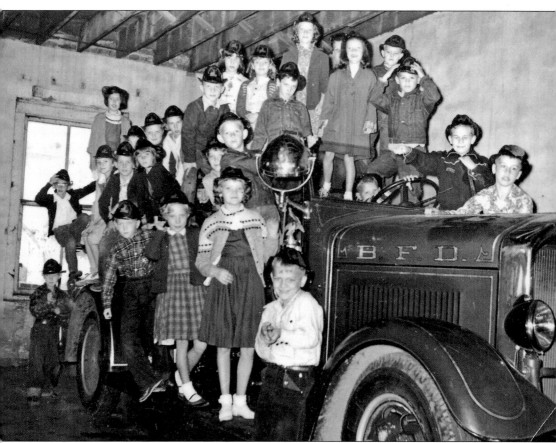

**CHILDREN POSE ON BOONE FIRE DEPARTMENT TRUCK.** These children are enjoying themselves around 1949 on a 1940s American LaFrance pumper truck operated by the Boone Fire Department. This particular truck pumped water at 500 gallons per minute, housed a 100-gallon booster tank, and carried hoses that reached more than 1,400 feet. The fire department owned one other vehicle at the time, a Ford truck that featured two 40-gallon chemical tanks and about 1,000 feet of hose. Also, during this time, the department employed one person, had 20 volunteers, operated out of one fire station, and was alarmed by sirens and the telephone. As the town of Boone grew, so did the number of buildings in the downtown area. The majority of structures in the town were wood framed and were constructed within close proximities to one another. To prevent a disaster, the town organized the first fire department in 1926. (Courtesy of Historic Boone.)

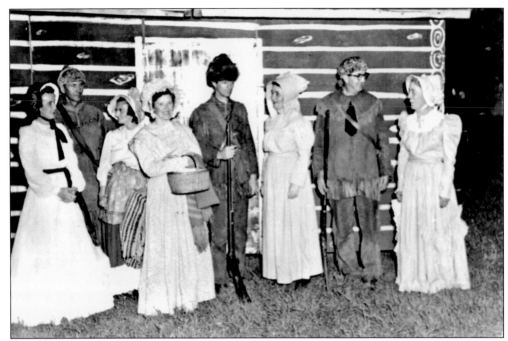

**WATAUGA CENTENNIAL CELEBRATION, 1949.** This photograph shows the outdoor pageant entitled *Echoes of the Blue Ridge*. The initial run of the outdoor pageant was hampered by rain and was restaged on June 30, 1950, on the athletic field of Appalachian State Teachers College. This second season of the pageant proved successful and, in turn, prompted a group of citizens to pursue a grander effort in staging *Horn in the West*. (Courtesy of Historic Boone.)

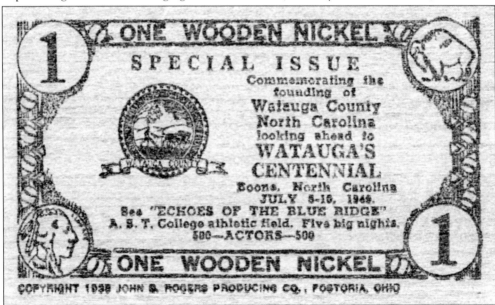

**WOODEN NICKEL FROM WATAUGA CENTENNIAL CELEBRATION.** This wooden currency was acceptable to all Watauga County merchants at the time of the celebration. The reverse side reads, "This Wooden Certificate is issued as a unique souvenir by the Watauga Centennial, Inc., in commemoration of the founding of Watauga County 100 Years Ago." (Courtesy of Brian Lambeth.)

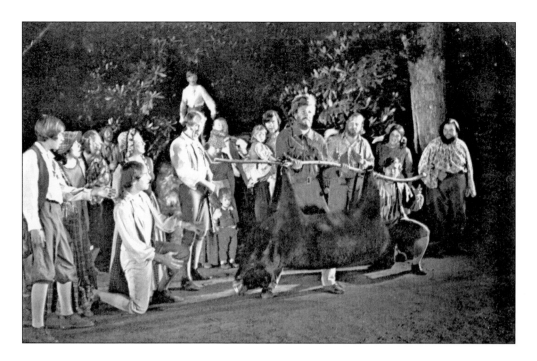

**HORN IN THE WEST.** Born of a pageant celebrating the centennial of Watauga County, *Horn in the West* has become one of the major outdoor dramas in the United States. The Southern Appalachian Historical Association produced the first show in June 1952. Playwright Kermit Hunter, renowned for writing outdoor historical dramas, was hired to write the script. These two scenes feature longtime cast member Glenn Causey, who portrayed Daniel Boone, holding a bear in a 1960s production (above) and a night scene during the first production in 1952 (below). (Above, courtesy of Richard Trexler; below, courtesy of Brian Lambeth.)

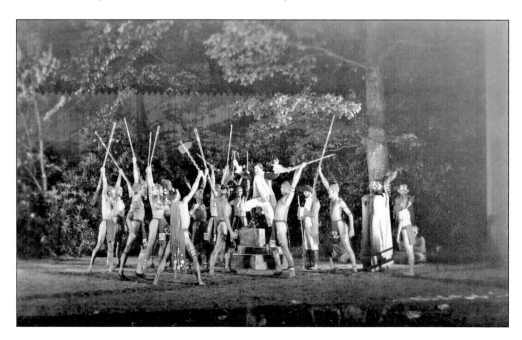

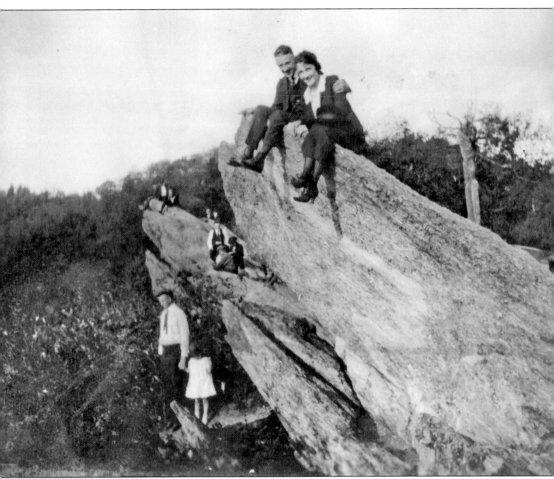

**THE BLOWING ROCK.** This c. 1920 photograph demonstrates the early popularity of the outcrop. This feature is the namesake for the town of Blowing Rock thus making it self-promotional. The rock is positioned at 4,090 feet above sea level and has a relative height of 3,000 feet from John's River Gorge below. Winds originating from far below the rock blow upwards, causing snow and other objects to "fall up." A 1950s promotional brochure states, "What goes down must come up!" and "Snow clouds above and the green depth below make an awe inspiring picture." The overlook features Hawksbill Mountain and Table Rock in the southwest, along with Grandfather Mountain and Mount Mitchell in the west. Pictured in the white shirt is Gordon Ballew (bottom), and the small girl in the white dress next to him is his daughter Mary Frances Ballew. (Courtesy of Byron and Sharon Tolbert.)

# BIBLIOGRAPHY

Arthur, John Preston. *A History of Watauga County North Carolina*. Johnson City, TN: Overmountain Press, 1915, reprinted 1992.

Corbitt, Tom, ed. *History of Development of Public Education in Watauga County, North Carolina*. Compiled by a bicentennial committee.

Dunlap, Bill and Tom Corbitt. *Remembrances*. 1974.

Green, Ivery. *A Disastrous Flood*. 1941.

McFarland, Betty. *Sketches of Early Watauga*. Boone Branch, American Association of University Women, 1973.

Whitener, Daniel J. *History of Watauga County A Souvenir of Watauga Centennial*. Boone, NC: 1949.

# www.arcadiapublishing.com

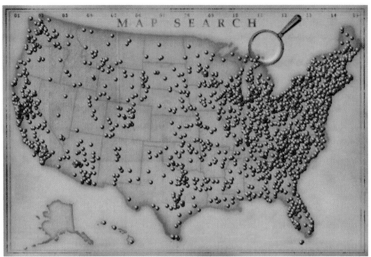

Discover books about the town where you grew up, the cities where your friends and families live, the town where your parents met, or even that retirement spot you've been dreaming about. Our Web site provides history lovers with exclusive deals, advanced notification about new titles, e-mail alerts of author events, and much more.

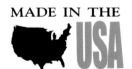

**MADE IN THE USA**

Arcadia Publishing, the leading local history publisher in the United States, is committed to making history accessible and meaningful through publishing books that celebrate and preserve the heritage of America's people and places. Consistent with our mission to preserve history on a local level, this book was printed in South Carolina on American-made paper and manufactured entirely in the United States.

This book carries the accredited Forest Stewardship Council (FSC) label and is printed on 100 percent FSC-certified paper. Products carrying the FSC label are independently certified to assure consumers that they come from forests that are managed to meet the social, economic, and ecological needs of present and future generations.

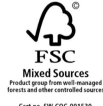

**FSC**
**Mixed Sources**
Product group from well-managed forests and other controlled sources

Cert no. SW-COC-001530
www.fsc.org
© 1996 Forest Stewardship Council

Find Your Place in History.